MANDATORY
MINIMUM DRUG SENTENCES

THROWING AWAY
THE KEY
OR THE
TAXPAYERS' MONEY?

JONATHAN P. CAULKINS
C. PETER RYDELL
WILLIAM L. SCHWABE
JAMES CHIESA

DRUG POLICY RESEARCH CENTER

RAND

PREFACE

In response to public concern over disparity of sentencing by judges and brevity of terms served by criminals, state legislatures and the Congress have written into law minimum sentences for specific crimes. In this report, we estimate the cost-effectiveness of mandatory minimum sentences for crimes related to cocaine distribution. These estimates are made relative to the cost-effectiveness of spending additional resources on enforcement without mandatory minimums and on drug treatment. Our central effectiveness measure is reduction of the nation's cocaine consumption, although we also examine reduction of cocaine-related crimes, along with decrease in cocaine spending, which is related to such crimes.

Because this report may be read by people with diverse interests, it is divided into two parts. Readers interested principally in narcotics-control and criminal-justice policy may wish to stop at the end of Part I. Part II has been prepared mainly for those also interested in the role and techniques of mathematical modeling in policy analysis, although some effort has been devoted to make it understandable to those not expert in this area.

This research was supported by a gift from Richard B. Wolf of Richland Mills and by funding from The Ford Foundation. This study was carried out within RAND's Drug Policy Research Center. The center's work is supported by The Ford Foundation, other foundations, government agencies, corporations, and individuals. It carries out extensive assessments of drug problems at local and national levels. Those interested in further information should contact the center at RAND's address on the inside front cover of this report.

CONTENTS

PART I

PART II

FIGURES

TABLES

In recent decades, the American public has responded favorably to political leaders and candidates who have espoused longer sentences for the possession and sale of drugs. Among the more popular sentencing extensions are "mandatory minimums," which require that a judge impose a sentence of at least a specified length if certain criteria are met. For example, federal law requires that a person convicted of possessing half a kilogram or more of cocaine powder be sentenced to at least five years in prison.

Mandatory minimums have enjoyed strong bipartisan support from elected representatives and presidential candidates. To these proponents, the certainty and severity of mandatory minimums make them better able to achieve incarceration's goals than are more flexible sentencing policies. Those goals include punishing the convicted and keeping them from committing more crimes for some period of time, as well as deterring others not in prison from committing similar crimes. Critics, however, worry that mandatory minimums foreclose discretionary judgment where it may most be needed, and they fear mandatory minimums result in instances of unjust punishment.

These are all important considerations, but mandatory minimums associated with drug crimes may also be viewed as a means of achieving the nation's drug control objectives. As such, how do they compare with other means? Do they contribute to the central objective—decreasing the nation's drug consumption and related consequences—at a cost that compares favorably with other approaches? In this report, we estimate how successful mandatory minimum sentences are, relative to other control strategies, at reducing drug consumption, drug-related crime, and the total flow of revenue through the cocaine market. The latter is a worthy objective in itself—America would be better off if money spent on drugs were spent on almost anything else—and it is also associated with drug-related crime.

We focus on cocaine, which many view as the most problematic drug in America today. We take two approaches to mathematically modeling the market for cocaine and arrive at the same basic conclusion: *Mandatory minimum sentences are not justifiable on the basis of cost-effectiveness at reducing cocaine consumption, cocaine expenditures, or drug-related crime.* Mandatory minimums reduce cocaine consumption less per million taxpayer dollars spent than does spending the same amount on enforcement under the previous sentencing regime. And either type of incarceration approach reduces drug consumption *less* than does putting heavy users through treatment programs, per million dollars spent. Similar results are obtained if the objective is to reduce spending on cocaine or cocaine-related crime. A principal reason for these findings is the high cost of incarceration. (Note these findings are limited to relative cost-effectiveness. As mentioned above, mandatory minimums have been justified—and criticized—on other grounds.)

REDUCING CONSUMPTION: MORE ENFORCEMENT AGAINST TYPICAL DEALERS

First, we estimate the cost-effectiveness of additional expenditures on enforcement against the average drug offender apprehended in the United States (whether that apprehension is by federal, state, or local authorities). In this approach, we track the flows of users among light-use, heavy-use, and no-use categories, and we analyze how overall cocaine market demand and supply respond to price. That is, if more money is spent on enforcement and incarceration, costs to dealers are increased, and so is the street price of cocaine; higher prices mean lower consumption. If more money is spent on treatment, consumption is reduced for most clients while they are in the program, and, for some, after they get out. We estimate the changes in total cocaine consumption over time for an additional million dollars invested in the alternatives considered. These changes, discounted to present value, are shown in Figure S.1.

The first two bars in the figure show the results of spending a million 1992 dollars[1] on additional enforcement by agencies at various levels of government against a representative sample of drug dealers. As shown by the first bar, if that money were used to extend to federal mandatory minimum lengths the sentences of dealers who would have been arrested anyway, U.S. cocaine consumption would be reduced by almost 13 kilograms. If, however, the money were used to arrest, confiscate the assets of, prosecute, and incarcerate

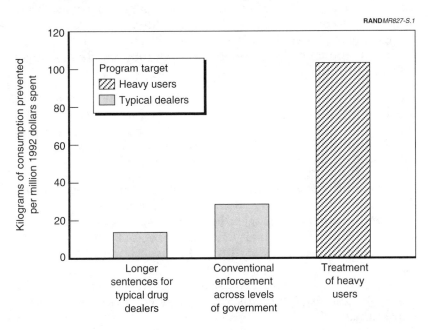

Figure S.1—Benefits of Alternative Cocaine Control Strategies

---

[1]All cost calculations in this report are in 1992 dollars. The choice of a reference year for cost figures is arbitrary. We choose 1992 to facilitate comparison with the results of earlier analyses. To convert costs in 1992 dollars to costs in 1996 dollars (the latest year for which inflation data are available), multiply by 1.119. To convert kilograms of cocaine consumption reduced per million 1992 dollars spent to kilograms reduced per million 1996 dollars spent, divide by 1.119.

more dealers (for prison terms of conventional length), cocaine consumption would be reduced by over 27 kilograms. Spending the million dollars treating heavy users would reduce cocaine consumption by a little over 100 kilograms.

Note we are estimating the impact of an *additional* million dollars. The results can be extrapolated to multiples thereof, but not to extremely large changes in spending. They certainly do not suggest that the most cost-effective approach is to shift all drug control resources from enforcement to treatment. Note also that we refer in the figure to "longer sentences" rather than to "mandatory minimums." Data on drug dealers arrested at state and local levels are insufficient to isolate those associated with drug amounts sufficient to trigger mandatory minimums. Instead, we analyze a hypothetical policy of applying the mandatory minimum sanction—longer sentences—to all convicted dealers.

The values shown are dependent, of course, on various assumptions we make. If the assumptions are changed, the values change. But for changes in assumptions over reasonable ranges, do the values change enough to make longer sentences more cost-effective than either of the other alternatives? We find they do not.

As an example, the values shown are dependent on the time horizon in which one is interested. The reason for this is as follows. When faced with extended sentences, drug dealers will want more income today to compensate them for the risk of increased prison time. As a result, cocaine prices will go up and consumption will go down. Benefits from reduced consumption will thus accrue immediately, while the costs of the extended prison terms will stretch out into the future. In contrast, if more users are treated this year, the costs accrue immediately, while the benefits in terms of reduced consumption by those who stay off cocaine stretch out into the future. Figure S.1 takes account of these different allocations of costs and benefits across future years in that future costs and benefits are discounted annually, out to 15 years—a time horizon typical in analyzing public policy. Beyond that point, any further costs and benefits count as zero. What if that terminal point were moved closer? What if one had not just a discounted interest in anything beyond the immediate future, but no interest? If the time horizon is set early enough, the effect is to "zero out" both the future stream of costs from mandatory minimums and the future benefits from treatment. Figure S.2 shows the relative cost-effectiveness of the three programs analyzed when time horizons are set at various points, from 1 to 15 years. At 15 years, the lines match the heights of the bars in Figure S.1. The time horizon must be reduced to only about three years before mandatory minimums look preferable to additional conventional enforcement, and close to two years before they look preferable to treatment. Hence, mandatory minimums appear cost-effective only to the highly myopic.

We also analyzed the implications of changing other assumptions. For example, dealers would want to be compensated for the increased risk of imprisonment they would incur in the event of increased enforcement. But the typical person would demand less compensation for being imprisoned five years from now than next year, and we assume drug dealers are even more "present-oriented." What would happen, though, if dealers wanted more risk compensa-

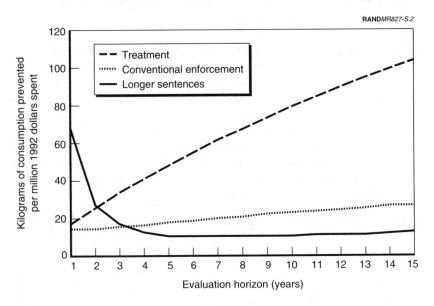

RAND*MR827-S.2*

Figure S.2—Benefits of Alternative Cocaine Control Strategies, for Different Time Horizons

tion, and if they discounted future costs less heavily than we assume? Longer sentences would seem more burdensome than we assume, dealers would demand a higher premium for handling cocaine, the price of cocaine would rise even more with increased enforcement spending, and consumption would fall even more. Consumption would also fall more than we expected if users were more responsive to price increases, i.e., if demand were more "elastic." We attempted to swing the balance toward extended incarceration by simultaneously increasing risk compensation by one-third, cutting the dealer discount rate by two-thirds, and increasing the elasticity of demand by 50 percent. The general profile of our results did indeed change. The cost-effectiveness of longer sentences tripled, while that of additional conventional enforcement doubled, and that of treatment rose by about a quarter. However, longer sentences remained the least cost-effective alternative, and treatment the most.

REDUCING CONSUMPTION: MORE ENFORCEMENT AGAINST HIGHER-LEVEL DEALERS

The first two bars in Figure S.1 represent enforcement approaches applied to a representative sample of all drug dealers arrested. Perhaps mandatory minimum sentences would be more cost-effective if they were restricted to somewhat higher-level dealers. By "higher-level dealers," we mean those who operate at higher levels of the drug distribution system, who make more money and thus have more to lose from more intensive enforcement. To approximate such a restriction, we limit the set of offenders analyzed to those who are prosecuted at the federal level and possess enough drugs to trigger a federal mandatory minimum sentence.

The results are shown in Figure S.3. There, the darkest bars represent the reduction in cocaine consumption from spending an additional million dollars in enforcement against the federal-level offenders just defined. The light bars are those from Figure S.1. Reading from the left, each light/dark pair of bars represents the same kind of program. The distribution of long sentences is the same for the first two bars, and the kinds of additional enforcement actions funded (arrest, seizure, prosecution, and incarceration for conventional sentence lengths) are the same for the next two bars.

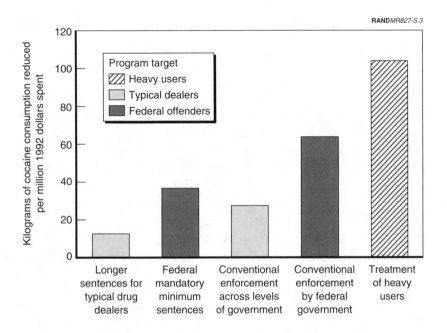

RAND*MR827-S.3*

Figure S.3—Benefits of Alternative Cocaine Control Strategies

As shown by the darker bars in Figure S.3, the consumption change achieved per million dollars spent on mandatory minimums is closer proportionately to that achieved through the other alternatives. While longer sentences for a representative set of all dealers have 46 percent of the effect of additional conventional enforcement against such dealers, federal mandatory minimums have 57 percent of the effect of additional conventional enforcement at the federal level. And, obviously, federal mandatory minimums do better relative to treating heavy users than do longer sentences for all dealers. To the higher-level dealers considered in this analysis, time in prison carries a greater cost, and amounts of cocaine and other assets seized through increased enforcement are also larger. Thus, risk compensation must be higher, and the higher resulting cocaine prices drive down consumption more. Nonetheless, at any given level of government, or against any given type of dealer, mandatory minimums are less cost-effective than conventional enforcement.

Why is that the case? Drug enforcement comprises two types of components, each of which is costly for taxpayers and each of which contributes to keeping drugs expensive: (1) arrest and conviction, which impose costs on suppliers principally through the seizure of drugs and other assets, and (2) incarceration of convicted defendants. Amid complaints about the "revolving door" of justice, some overlook that arrest and conviction impose costs on dealers. In fact, on average, arrest and conviction impose greater costs on dealers per taxpayer dollar spent than does incarcerating dealers. Since mandatory minimums alter the mix of these two components of enforcement in favor of incarceration, they dilute or reduce the efficiency of enforcement relative to simply expanding both components proportionately.

As with the light bars, the precise heights of the dark bars in Figure S.3 depend on various assumptions. Again, these include assumptions about such uncertain values as the compensation dealers would demand for increased imprisonment risk, the rate at which dealers discount future costs, the responsiveness of buyers to shifts in cocaine prices, what it costs to arrest a dealer, and the value of drugs and other assets seized. To test the sensitivity of our results to these assumptions, we vary the assumed values of factors such as these one at a time over substantial ranges. In all cases, conventional enforcement is more cost-effective than mandatory minimums, and treatment is more than twice as cost-effective as mandatory minimums. Even when assumed values are varied two at a time, large departures from assumed values are required for mandatory minimums to be the most cost-effective approach. In Figure S.4, for example, the government's cost of arresting a dealer and the compensation a dealer wants for risking a year of imprisonment are varied simultaneously. The star shows the values assumed for the results in Figure S.3. As Figure S.4 shows, mandatory minimums would be the most cost-effective alternative only if arrest costs were to exceed $30,000 and a dealer were to value his time at some $250,000 or more per year. Such dollar values would typify only those dealers at a fairly high level in the cocaine trade and who are unusually difficult to ar-

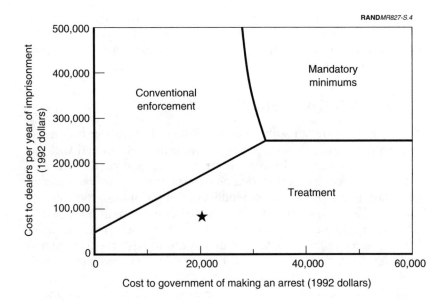

Figure S.4—Which Program Is More Cost-Effective at Reducing Cocaine
Consumption Under Different Assumptions?

rest.[2] For dealers costing less to arrest, cocaine control dollars would
be better spent on further conventional enforcement. For dealers
demanding less risk compensation, the money would be better spent
treating heavy users than on enforcement against such dealers.

Long sentences could thus be a smart strategy if selectively applied.
Unfortunately, because mandatory minimum sentences are triggered by quantity possessed and because those thresholds are low,
they are not selectively applied to high-level dealers. (Indeed, anecdotal evidence suggests that high-level dealers can sometimes avoid
mandatory minimums more easily than their subordinates. High-
level dealers have more knowledge about their organization to use as
bargaining chips with prosecutors. Furthermore, such dealers often

---

[2]Even for these dealers, it is possible that conventional enforcement would be more
cost-effective than mandatory minimums. That would be the case if the range of conventional sentences could be matched to the range of offenders so that the highest-
level dealers received very long sentences.

do not physically possess their drugs, as is required for a mandatory minimum to take effect; they hire others to incur that risk. To the extent that this occurs, mandatory minimum sentences would be even less effective than these results suggest.)

REDUCING COCAINE-RELATED CRIME

Of course, cocaine consumption is not the only measure of interest. Many Americans are worried about the crime associated with cocaine production, distribution, and use. Using data on the causes of drug-related crime and our cocaine market analysis, we quantify the approximate crime reduction benefits of the various alternatives. We find no difference between conventional enforcement and mandatory minimums in relation to property crime; the former, however, should reduce crimes against persons by about 70 percent more than the latter. But treatment should reduce serious crimes (against persons as well as property) the most per million dollars spent—on the order of 15 times as much as the incarceration alternatives would.

Why do we get these results? Most drug-related crime is economically motivated—undertaken, e.g., to procure money to support a habit or to settle scores between rival dealers. Fewer crimes are the direct result of drug consumption—crimes committed "under the influence." However, we find very little difference between conventional enforcement and mandatory minimums in their effects on the money flowing through the market, and thus very little difference in their effects on economically motivated crime. We do find, as shown in Figure S.3, appreciable differences in consumption effects, and thus appreciable differences in effects on crimes committed under the influence. The latter are more likely than are economically motivated crimes to be crimes against persons.

Treatment, however, has an enormous advantage over enforcement in reducing the economic value of the cocaine market—larger even than that shown in Figure S.3 for reducing cocaine consumption. Why is that? When a treated offender stays off drugs, that means less money flowing into the market. But when a dealer facing the risk of a longer sentence raises his price, say one percent, to compensate, buyers will reduce the amount of cocaine they purchase. The best evidence suggests that reduction will be something on the order of one percent. Thus, the total revenue flowing through the cocaine market stays about the same, and so do the incentives for economically motivated drug-related crimes. Therefore, the effect of the enforcement alternatives is limited almost entirely to the relatively small number of crimes committed under the influence. Treatment, however, has an advantage against those crimes similar to that shown in Figure S.3 and an even greater advantage against the larger number of economically motivated crimes.

CONCLUSION

Long sentences for serious crimes have intuitive appeal. They respond to deeply held beliefs about punishment for evil actions, and in many cases they ensure that, by removing a criminal from the streets, further crimes that would have been committed will not be. But in the case of black-market crimes like drug dealing, a jailed supplier is often replaced by another supplier if demand remains. And not all agree whether mandatory minimums satisfy American standards of fairness and justice. Even those who believe they do must ask themselves to what extent might it be desirable to give up some punishment of the guilty to gain some further reduction in cocaine consumption—consumption that can victimize the innocent. This trade of punishment for drug use reduction must be considered because long sentences are expensive and cocaine control resources are limited. As we show, if reducing consumption or violence is the goal, more can be achieved by spending additional money arresting, prosecuting, and sentencing dealers to standard prison terms than by spending it sentencing (fewer) dealers to longer, mandatory terms. (And that is to say nothing of what might be achieved by redirecting resources from enforcement to treatment—admittedly, a more difficult reallocation because those programs might be run by completely different agencies.) We find an exception in the case of the highest-level dealers—those who value their time most highly and are hardest to apprehend—where sentences of mandatory minimum length appear to be the most cost-effective approach. However, current mandatory minimum laws are not focused on those dealers.

ACKNOWLEDGMENTS

We are grateful to Richard B. Wolf for the generous gift to the Drug Policy Research Center that made this work possible. We also thank the DPRC Advisory Board members who helped develop the RAND Drug Policy Forum in Washington, D.C., which served as the impetus for Mr. Wolf's gift. We have benefited from the support of our colleagues Susan Everingham and Peter Reuter, who reviewed a draft of this study and contributed in substantial ways to whatever degree of consistency and clarity the reader may judge us to have achieved. We also benefited from comments and suggestions from Allan Abrahamse and Peter Greenwood.

Chapter One

INTRODUCTION

It has become evident from Americans' response to pollsters and to candidates and initiatives that they do not view prisons as "correctional institutions." Instead, the public looks to prisons to punish criminals, keep them isolated from society, and in so doing deter others from following a life of crime. The principal means of achieving these objectives has been longer prison sentences, and a favored way of assuring a long term has been the mandatory minimum—a sentence required by statute when specified criteria have been met.

Mandatory minimums have had strong bipartisan support from elected representatives and presidential candidates (Schulhofer, 1993). To these proponents, the certainty and severity of mandatory minimums make them better able to achieve incarceration's goals than are more flexible sentencing policies. Proponents also argue that the threat of a mandatory minimum can induce a plea to a lesser charge and put the offender away for a while without the cost of a trial. Critics, however, worry that mandatory minimums foreclose discretionary judgment where it may most be needed, and they fear such laws result in instances of unjust punishment.

We do not take sides in this debate, though we undertake a qualitative, critical review of claims in favor of (and against) mandatory minimums (see Chapter Two). Instead, we attempt here to provide another piece of information relevant for forming opinions about mandatory minimums by asking, How well do they work? Of course that depends on the definition of "work."

In this report, we attempt to determine how well mandatory minimums "work" at controlling illegal drugs. In the context of the drug market, mandatory minimums might be said to "work" if they fulfill what Barry McCaffrey, director of the Office of National Drug Control Policy, has called "our central purpose and mission—reducing illicit drug use and its consequences."[1] We would expect that, *all other things equal*, imposing longer sentences for drug law violations will reduce drug use. But in the real world, all other things are never equal. If we expend resources incarcerating drug dealers for extended periods, we will have fewer resources left to do other things. For example, if we paid for longer prison sentences by forgoing opportunities to expand drug use prevention, it is no longer clear whether drug use would go up or down. The outcome would depend on whether spending a dollar on mandatory minimum sentences does more or less to reduce drug consumption than spending a dollar on prevention.

The quantity of benefits produced per dollar spent on a program is called its cost-effectiveness. Hence, a more instructive rephrasing of the common question concerning mandatory minimum sentences is, "Are mandatory minimum sentences more cost-effective at reducing drug consumption than other available alternatives?"

Ideally one would answer this question by quantitatively estimating the cost-effectiveness of every conceivable drug control program. Practically that is a formidable task, so we compare mandatory minimum sentences to just two prominent alternatives: (1) conventional enforcement and sentencing and (2) expanding drug treatment. We choose the latter because earlier work (Rydell and Everingham, 1994) found it to be the most cost-effective of four programs considered (the other three were source country control, interdiction en route, and enforcement within the United States). However, it may not be as practical to transfer resources from budgets supporting mandatory minimum policies to those supporting treatment as it may be to those implementing some other enforcement strategy. Thus, as our principal alternative we use additional enforcement inside U.S. borders with conventional sentencing—a

---

[1]Letter from Barry R. McCaffrey, April 29, 1996, accompanying *The National Drug Control Strategy: 1996,* Office of National Drug Control Policy, Executive Office of the President, Washington, D.C., 1996.

well-defined option and the second most cost-effective in the Rydell-Everingham study.[2] We restrict ourselves to the control of cocaine—the most problematic drug in the United States by most measures, and the drug for which the best data are available. However, we suspect similar conclusions might apply as well to heroin.

We take two distinct mathematical modeling approaches to comparing cost-effectiveness, for two reasons. First, the use of two approaches permits more confidence in the results (since the results are similar). Second, the two approaches have different strengths and, although each addresses the same central cost-effectiveness questions, they contribute different perspectives.

One of the approaches applies to enforcement against the typical drug dealer apprehended, whether at the federal, state, or local level (see Chapters Three and Six). This adaptation of a previously developed approach (Everingham and Rydell, 1994; Rydell and Everingham, 1994) translates additional enforcement into greater dealer risks and costs and higher prices in the cocaine market. It tracks the flows of cocaine consumers among light-use, heavy-use, and no-use categories and explains the manner in which overall cocaine market demand and supply respond to price. This model estimates changes in total cocaine consumption over time for every additional million dollars invested in the cocaine control alternatives considered.

Although comprehensive and dynamic, this first approach cannot focus on particular segments of the market. Therefore, we have developed for this study a second model, which, although static and thus unable to track time trends, is more flexible and detailed. We apply it only to offenders prosecuted at the federal level who possess enough cocaine to trigger federal mandatory minimum sentences. We make such a restriction partly because mandatory minimums might be more cost-effective if targeted to higher-level offenders (as will become apparent in Chapter Three).

---

[2]This option does not include user sanctions or financial investigations of "money laundering." Nor does it include enforcement against dealers outside of the United States: controlling coca production and processing in source countries and interdicting shipments en route to U.S. wholesalers. Rydell and Everingham (1994) found the source-country and interdiction approaches to be less effective than conventional enforcement (there called "domestic enforcement").

The "central purpose" cited by McCaffrey is to reduce not only drug use but also its consequences. A principal consequence is, of course, drug-related crime and violence. We take two approaches to a rough assessment of whether mandatory minimums serve to reduce such crime and violence. In one approach, we estimate the money flowing through the drug market, under the assumption that money flows are related to crime and violence. Secondly, we directly estimate changes in drug-related crime levels (see Chapter Four).

Our analyses suggest that, in reducing consumption, conventional enforcement without mandatory minimum sentencing is about half again as cost-effective as enforcement with mandatory minimums. Treatment is even more cost-effective. Conventional enforcement is also more cost-effective than mandatory minimums at reducing cocaine-related violence, although the two enforcement approaches are about equally effective at reducing cocaine market revenues per million program dollars spent. Again, treatment is much more cost-effective at achieving both those objectives.

We present these findings and their sensitivity to changes in our assumptions, together with a brief summary of our analytic approach, in Part I of this report. Part II documents our methodology in detail and repeats the results tables, accompanied by some further interpretive observations. The reader principally interested in our findings and their meaning may wish to read only Part I.

PART I

Chapter Two

THE LAWS AND THE SURROUNDING DEBATE

Among the various issues that must be taken into account in deciding to expand or cut back the application of mandatory minimum laws, we address only one, but we believe it a central one: their cost-effectiveness at achieving national drug and crime control goals. Naturally, our findings in that regard are best interpreted in the context of the other issues. In this chapter, for the benefit of the reader unfamiliar with mandatory minimums and the claims made by their proponents and opponents, we describe the following:

- The origin and nature of mandatory minimum sentencing.

- The case for mandatory minimums in terms of the goals such sentencing is intended to achieve, together with objections that have been made about whether such goals are likely to be achieved.

- Various other objections to the statutes over unintended or unwise consequences.

The discussion in this chapter is generally qualitative. It raises serious questions about mandatory minimums and the way they are implemented. If the tone seems, on balance, critical—that reflects the bulk of what has been written. However, we do not intend an overall negative judgment on the basis of this chapter alone. It could be argued that the alleged shortcomings should not be allowed to obscure the contribution that mandatory minimums make to the nation's drug control efforts. That contribution is what we address in the remainder of the report.

To put mandatory minimum sentences in context, we briefly review the recent history of sentencing prior to the establishment of such minimums. We then elaborate on the mandatory minimum concept and how it is implemented, particularly with respect to cocaine-related offenses, which are the subject of the analysis in the following chapters. To keep this chapter to a manageable length, we restrict ourselves largely to federal mandatory minimum laws. In discussing sentencing disparity, we treat briefly the distribution and variation of mandatory minimums across states.

RECENT HISTORY OF FEDERAL SENTENCING REFORM

U.S. drug control policy has a long and varied history. Musto (1973, 1989, and 1991) reviews the fluctuating historical and epidemiological context of control policy. Gerstein and Harwood (1990, p. 43) summarize the major control enthusiasms as libertarian (at the end of the last century), medical treatment (beginning of this century), and criminal justice sanctions (mid-century to present). At any given time, of course, all three ideas inform public policy: Only the proportions in the mix change. Gawin and Ellinwood (1988) discuss the medical point of view. Reuter (1992) discusses the current dominance of the punitive approach to drug control. Here, we limit ourselves to the period of criminal-justice sanctions.

Indeterminate Sentencing

Through the middle part of the 20th century, the rehabilitation model of punishment and indeterminate sentencing was the norm in the United States. Judges determined whether people convicted of crimes would be sentenced to prison and, if so, for how long. Parole boards determined both when prison inmates were ready for release and whether behavior of parolees warranted return to prison (Forst, 1995, p. 375).

This flexibility in sentencing was consistent with the notion of rehabilitation—that punishment could reform offenders (hence the terms "corrections" and "correctional institutions") and that agents of the system could judge the capacity for reform and the extent to which individuals had been reformed.

Sentencing Guidelines

In the 1980s, after a decade of studying the rehabilitation model of punishment and indeterminate sentencing, the Congress and many state legislatures concluded that the system was outmoded and in need of reform. The system lacked the certainty necessary to inspire public confidence and operate as a meaningful deterrent to crime. An unjustifiable variation existed in the sentences imposed by judges on similarly situated defendants. At the federal level, the U.S. Parole Commission compounded the problem by releasing prisoners according to its own view of the appropriate term of imprisonment. In response, judges began to factor into sentences the anticipated actions of the Parole Commission (Hatch, 1993, pp. 187–188).

The federal Sentencing Reform Act (SRA) of 1984 created a Sentencing Commission to develop sentencing guidelines. The objectives of sentencing as announced in the SRA were

- to reflect the seriousness of the offense, to promote respect for the law, and to provide just punishment

- to afford adequate deterrence to criminal conduct

- to protect the public from further crimes of the defendant

- to provide the defendant with educational or vocational training, medical care, or other correctional treatment (Hatch, p. 188).

The sentencing guidelines went into effect in 1987, ending the federal parole system and establishing a system of appellate sentence review (Forst, 1995, p. 377).

Mandatory Minimum Sentences

Since 1984, the Congress has enacted an array of mandatory minimum penalties specifically targeted at drugs and violent crime (Hatch, 1993). In 1986, the Congress significantly altered sentencing policy by focusing on drug trafficking and distribution offenses and by tying the minimum penalty to the gross weight of drugs involved in the offense. Substantial mandatory sentence enhancements for using or carrying a firearm during a crime of violence were also enacted. Additional mandatory minimums were imposed for drug offenders who sold drugs to minors or who possessed certain weapons during commission of the offense. In 1988, the Congress prescribed mandatory minimum penalties for conspiracies to commit certain offenses and a mandatory minimum of five years imprisonment was imposed for simple possession of "crack" cocaine (Hatch, 1993, pp. 192–193).

Mandatory minimum sentences for simple possession of controlled substances are specified by 21 U.S.C. § 844. Mandatory minimums for manufacturing, distributing, dispensing, or possession with intent to manufacture, distribute, or dispense controlled substances are specified by 21 U.S.C. § 841.

These two code sections, together with a third covering trade in controlled substances, are responsible for the bulk of federal mandatory sentences (see Appendix A for pertinent text of the three laws). From 1984 through August of 1990, 59,780 cases were sentenced pursuant to the 60 federal statutes containing mandatory minimum sentencing provisions. Of these, the three statutes prescribing mandatory minimum sentences for drug offenses account for 91 percent of the convictions (see Table 2.1).

Controlled substances include heroin, cocaine, phencyclidine (PCP), lysergic acid diethyl amide (LSD), marijuana, and methamphetamine. Here, we restrict our discussion to cocaine.

Table 2.1

Statutes Responsible for Federal Mandatory Minimum Convictions, January 1984 Through August 1990

Code section	Subject	Number of mandatory min. cases	Percentage of total
21 U.S.C. §841	Manufacture and distribution of controlled substances	38,214	64
21 U.S.C. §844	Possession of controlled substances	10,218	17
21 U.S.C. §960	Penalties for import or export of controlled substances	6,135	10
All others		5,213	9
Total		59,780	100

The federal mandatory minimums for cocaine offenses are summarized in Table 2.2. Sentences depend on four factors:

- The weight of the mixture containing a detectable amount of the controlled substance.

- Whether the detected substance is powder or crack cocaine.

- The number of prior federal or state drug felony convictions.

- Whether it is a matter of simple possession or possession with intent to manufacture, distribute, or dispense. (The penalties in the body of Table 2.2 apply to offenses more serious than simple possession.)

Federal mandatory minimum sentences range from 15 days to life imprisonment without parole. Actual sentences may be higher than minimum and may be augmented by fines and up to 10 years of supervision after release.

FULFILLMENT OF OBJECTIVES

Mandatory minimum sentences were meant to achieve the following objectives (U.S. Sentencing Commission, 1991, pp. 14–15):

Table 2.2

Federal Mandatory Minimum Sentences for Cocaine Offenses

| | Grams of Mixture (Prior Drug Felony Convictions) | |
Sentence	Powder	Crack
None	> 0 gm (None)	Same
15 days	> 0 gm (One)	Same
90 days	> 0 gm (Two or more)	Same
5 years	≥ 500 gm (None)	≥ 5 gm (None)[a]
10 years	≥ 500 gm (One or more)	≥ 5 gm (One or more)
	≥ 5000 gm (None)	≥ 50 gm (None)
20 years	≥ 5000 gm (One)	≥ 50 gm (One)
Life	≥ 5000 gm (Two or more)	≥ 50 gm (Two or more)

[a]There are also five-year mandatory minimum crack sentences for simple possession of more than 5 grams (no prior convictions), more than 3 grams (one prior), and more than 1 gram (two or more priors).

1. Retribution or "just deserts."

2. Deterrence.

3. Incapacitation, especially of the serious offender.

4. Elimination of sentencing disparity.

5. Inducement of cooperation.

6. Inducement of pleas.

Here, we consider each of these objectives. We examine the intent, arguments about whether mandatory minimums are or are not likely to achieve the intent, and any available evidence.

Retribution or "Just Deserts"

Mandatory minimum sentencing arose out of public belief that people arrested for felonies are not being sufficiently punished. In particular, many people think that, given discretion, judges do not impose long enough sentences on convicted criminals, and that criminals do not serve a sufficient part of the sentences they do receive. Using sample data drawn from the 1985 cohort of defendants sentenced in the federal system, the U.S. Sentencing Commission attempted to separate impacts of three sets of sentencing provisions: the sentencing guidelines, the career offender provisions of the Sentencing Reform Act of 1984, and mandatory minimums imposed by the Anti-Drug Abuse Act of 1986. For drug offenses, they assumed an average pre-guideline time served of 23.1 months and estimated an additional average time of 0.9 months due to the sentencing guidelines, 8.7 months due to career criminal provisions, and 25.0 months due to mandatory minimums. Thus, mandatory minimums were estimated to more than double the average time served for federal drug offenses, to 57.7 months[1] (U.S. Sentencing Commission, 1991, p. 114).

---

[1]Nevertheless, the U.S. Sentencing Commission was unwilling to acknowledge mandatory minimums as superior to the guidelines, concluding that guidelines appear to serve the purpose of "just deserts" better, because they are informed by consideration of hundreds of actual offenses and allow for fine distinctions in offense severity (U.S. Sentencing Commission, 1991, p. 33).

Deterrence

Imprisonment is intended to deter the individual who is sentenced from further involvement in crime (specific deterrence) and, by example, to discourage other people from committing similar offenses (general deterrence). Deterrence is said to depend in part on certainty of punishment. By making minimum sentences mandatory, punishment accompanying conviction is meant to be more certain. Thus, in theory, mandatory minimum drug penalties should enhance deterrence effects (U.S. Sentencing Commission, 1991, pp. 14, 33–34).

However, there are practical impediments to this. First, if mandatory minimums induce prosecutors to accept more pleas of guilty to a lesser charge, the deterrent effect upon others is weakened. It has also been argued that the punishment resulting in mandatory minimums is less certain than from following sentencing guidelines because the former considers only the offense charged, while the latter also considers the real offense committed (U.S. Sentencing Commission, pp. 33–34).

More fundamentally, deterrence is of limited effect against black-market crimes. To see why, consider first a nonconsensual crime like burglary. The benefit accruing to the burglar is not affected by sentencing severity, while longer, mandatory sentences would increase the burglar's expected cost. Thus, longer sentences might result in costs exceeding benefits for some offenders, thereby deterring some burglaries.

But the benefits of selling drugs are different. They are not independent of the expected sentence. As the expected sentence (and thus the nonmonetary cost to dealers) increases, so does the markup in drug price (because the dealer would want to be compensated for his risk), so the benefit of selling drugs increases. Extending sentences thus increases not only the expected nonmonetary cost in terms of the time spent in prison but also the expected monetary reward of dealing. It is thus not clear that extended sentences will deter drug dealing. (However, they might affect who chooses to deal. Presumably, tougher sentences will select for dealers who attach high value to money and low value to the risk of lengthy incarceration.)

Incapacitation, Especially of the Serious Offender

Proponents of mandatory minimums argue that they increase public safety by incapacitating drug dealers and violent criminals for extended periods of time (U.S. Sentencing Commission, p. 14). Under 21 U.S.C. § 848(b), a person organizing or supervising a continuing criminal enterprise dealing in large drug quantities—a "kingpin"—is subject to a mandatory minimum sentence of life imprisonment.

However, there are four ways the intent of the law may be thwarted by operation of the system in practice. First, kingpins may be in a better position to avoid mandatory minimums through cooperation with prosecutors than are their underlings, who have less knowledge regarding drug operations to barter for a more lenient sentence.

Second, the fundamental limitations of incapacitation to control black-market activities are even more severe than are the limitations on deterrence. While the incarcerated dealer can no longer sell drugs, that does not mean a smaller quantity of drugs is being sold. The common pessimism is not too far from the truth: "If you arrest one dealer, someone else will take his or her place." Incarcerating a violent criminal might reduce the total number of violent crimes since there is very little *demand* for violent crime. But there is a demand for drugs, and there is a very large number of people willing to sell drugs, provided sufficient remuneration.

Third, mandatory minimums have to be considered in light of their place within the entire U.S. incarceration system. That is, it is necessary to consider not only those incarcerated under mandatory minimums, but those who must be freed because of them. In some states, the number of convicted felons is growing so fast that other criminals must be released early to make room for the newly sentenced. Mandatory minimums essentially give inmates sentenced under them a priority in holding prison space. Are these drug offenders the criminals who should be held in the event of a court-ordered early release? Should violent felons really be let go first?[2]

Fourth, mandatory minimums are additive—someone convicted of two counts subject to mandatory minimum sentencing receives

---

[2]For a quantitative treatment of some of these issues, see Cohen et al., forthcoming.

twice the minimum sentence. Under the sentencing guidelines, sentencing is incremental—someone convicted of two counts receives less than twice the sentence of someone convicted of just one (U.S. Sentencing Commission, 1991, p. 31). Additive mandatory minimums can result in very long sentences that keep offenders in prison well beyond the point at which they would have stopped committing crimes (the typical criminal career does not last more than 10 or 15 years).[3] Again, critics charge that crime, and particularly violent crime, would be reduced more if the prison space these offenders occupy were allocated to younger, more violent felons.

Elimination of Sentencing Disparity

It is argued that mandatory minimums reduce disparity in sentencing between offenders who have committed similar crimes. Before mandatory minimums, it was possible for someone convicted of a serious drug offense to receive a short term from a sympathetic judge, while someone else convicted of a similar crime got a longer term from a tougher judge. Now, with the lower end of the sentencing range effectively eliminated, mandatory minimum proponents hold that offenders committing similar crimes must get similarly long sentences.

It is countered that any reduction in this kind of disparity is at least partially offset by increases in others. For example, the crafters of mandatory minimums have attempted to reduce unwarranted disparity by basing the sentences on a small number of key factors: amount of mixture in possession, type of mixture (crack or powder), and number of prior drug felony convictions. However, these omit many important factors that can be taken into account within the sentencing ranges permitted by the guidelines. Among the most important of those factors are intent to break the law, importance of the offender's role in the drug dealing operation, and position in the overall drug commerce hierarchy. None of these is necessarily represented by factors such as amount in possession or number of priors. In particular, dealers above the lower market levels often go to great lengths to avoid being in physical possession of the drugs they own.

---

[3]See Greenwood et al. (1994) for a quantitative analysis of the costs and benefits of long prison sentences.

They hire others, sometimes known as "mules" or "couriers," to pick up, hold, and transport their drugs. As a result of failure to recognize important distinctions between cases, excessive disparity in sentencing may be replaced by what Schulhofer (1993, p. 210) calls "excessive uniformity."

Despite their general leveling effect, mandatory minimums can actually increase sentencing disparities in some cases. For example, as the U.S. Sentencing Commission (1991, p. 31) points out, the law provides for large sentencing step-ups or "cliffs" over tiny quantity ranges. A first-time offender found to be in possession of 5.1 grams of crack must be sentenced to at least 5 years in prison. But a first-time offender found to be in possession of 5.0 grams of crack misses the mandatory minimum criterion and can be imprisoned for at most one year. Thus, these two very similar offenders draw sentences differing by at least four years. (Of course, any sentencing regime based at least partly on amounts possessed is likely to include such step-ups. But sentencing guidelines allow for smaller and more numerous steps or ranges that may overlap, and they allow other factors to be considered within those ranges.)

Mandatory minimums are also intended to override judicial discretion, which has been perceived as giving rise to unwarranted disparities in sentencing. However, prosecutors can still bring different charges in similar cases. For example, prosecutors may move to reduce a charge in exchange for information. Furthermore, prosecutors may vary in their charging practices based on the degree to which they account for other factors not explicitly considered in establishing mandatory minimums. For example, instead of charging a suspect under a count carrying a mandatory minimum, a prosecutor can in some cases charge a suspect with use of a communications facility to further a drug offense (the so-called "phone count"). Another possibility is to charge the suspect with simple possession of a controlled substance (Schulhofer, 1993, p. 206). By any of these means, prosecutors can induce sentencing disparity between cases that may not vary in the facts as much as others do for which judges are not permitted the same discretion.

Although our discussion focuses on federal mandatory minimums, we should note that the broad goal of reducing or eliminating disparity in sentencing for similar offenses depends on state, as well as federal, sentencing. At present, there is considerable disparity in state mandatory minimum sentences for cocaine sale and trafficking. Figure 2.1 shows some of these sentences for selling cocaine (note both scales are logarithmic and the two-letter postal abbreviations for the states are used). If standards for mandatory minimums were consistent from state to state, the symbols of the different states (for identical priors, e.g., GA2, CT2, WA2) would lie on the same diagonal line indicating longer sentences for larger amounts. Clearly, they do not. Nevada, for example, mandates a one-year sentence for the sale of any amount of cocaine by a first-time offender; the analogous sentence in Delaware is six years; in Connecticut, fifteen years. Georgia mandates a life sentence for the sale of any amount of cocaine—even a few grams—if the seller had previously been convicted of a felony; in Michigan, the sale must amount to at least 50 grams if a life sentence is to be required for a second-time offender. But Michigan is severe compared to neighboring Wisconsin. If a man traveling with

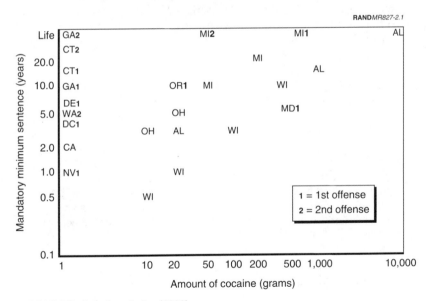

SOURCE: Data from Leiter (1993).

Figure 2.1—Some Mandatory Minimum Sentences for Selling Various Amounts of Cocaine, by State

60 grams of cocaine stops and sells it in Marinette, Wisconsin, he is subject to a minimum of a year in prison if caught and convicted. If he waits until he is a few miles up the road and sells it in Menominee, Michigan, he is subject to a 10-year mandatory minimum if caught and convicted—or life in prison if it is a second offense.

Inducement of Cooperation

Lengthy mandatory minimum sentences provide a stick for inducing cooperation in investigating and prosecuting others involved in the drug trade. The carrot is 10 U.S.C. § 3553(e), which authorizes a judge to impose a sentence below the mandatory minimum if the government makes a motion for a lower sentence on the basis of a defendant's substantial assistance in the investigation or prosecution of others. This provision has been used with some frequency. A General Accounting Office study (1993) found that in 15 percent of cases involving offenders convicted of violating a federal statute carrying a mandatory minimum, the sentence imposed was less than the minimum because the defendant was found to have offered "substantial assistance."

This provision, however, can conflict with the public interest (expressed through special provisions for "kingpins") in meting out the longest sentences to those most heavily involved in the drug trade. As Schulhofer (1993, p. 212) puts it,

> Defendants who are most in the know, and thus have the most "substantial assistance" to offer, are often those who are most centrally involved in conspiratorial crimes. . . . Minor players, peripherally involved and with little knowledge or responsibility, have little to offer and thus can wind up with far more severe sentences than the boss.

Inducement of Pleas

Guilty defendants may wish to plead guilty to a lesser offense to avoid risking drawing a longer sentence if charged, tried, and convicted of an offense carrying a mandatory minimum sentence. Such guilty pleas would save the cost of a trial.

> In this context, the value of a mandatory minimum sentence lies not in its imposition, but in its value as a bargaining chip to be given away in return for the resource-saving plea from the defendant to a more leniently sanctioned charge (U.S. Sentencing Commission, 1991, p. 15).

However, when the prosecutor does not wish to bargain, mandatory minimums can actually cost more money by prompting defendants to demand a jury trial, with the chance of acquittal, rather than pleading guilty to a charge carrying a mandatory minimum.[4] It is unclear which effect dominates.

OTHER ISSUES IN THE CURRENT DEBATE

Here, we largely leave aside the question of whether mandatory minimums will fulfill their goals and focus instead on provisions of the statutes that lead to outcomes that appear unintended or unwise.

Treating Crack Differently from Powder

Crack, a smokable base form of cocaine, has been singled out for severe punishment under mandatory minimum legislation. The quantity of cocaine triggering a mandatory minimum sentence varies by a factor of 100 depending on the form of the drug. For a five-year minimum, it is 5 grams of crack or 500 grams of powder. For a 10-year minimum, it is 10 times each: 50 grams of crack or 5,000 grams of powder.

Because crack is smoked, whereas insufflation is the most common mode of administration for powder cocaine, it produces a particularly rapid, intense euphoria. It is a well-known principle of psychology that more rapid feedback tends to be more habit-forming, so crack induces compulsive use more readily than powder cocaine. That mandatory minimum legislation was passed at the peak of pub-

---

[4]In the first calendar year following the passage of California's "three strikes" mandatory minimum sentencing law for repeat offenders, Los Angeles County's superior courts experienced a 25 percent increase in jury trials (Countywide Criminal Justice Coordination Committee, 1995).

lic fear about crack may also help account for the severity of sanctions against this form of the drug.

However, crack is typically produced from powder cocaine in small batches. Thus, a cocaine wholesaler who deals in lots of one pound quantities of powder cocaine (454 grams) is not subject to any mandatory minimum sentence. But he or she might sell to, say, eight lower-level dealers who each has a couple of ounces (56 grams) in stock. These in turn might each sell to eight street-level dealers who "rock up" cocaine into crack a couple of "eight balls" (or eighths of an ounce) at a time. The original pound of powder would thus supply 64 street-level dealers with two-eighths of an ounce of powder cocaine each, which they then turn into a like quantity of crack. These 64 street-level dealers would be subject to federal mandatory minimum sentences, even though their suppliers and their suppliers' wholesale supplier two distribution levels above them are not.[5]

The powder/crack distinction also raises the specter of racially correlated sentencing disparities. More than 90 percent of defendants are African American in crack cocaine cases, compared with slightly over 25 percent in cases involving powder.[6]

But are crack cases in practice more likely to draw mandatory sentences than powder cases? The two upper pie charts in Figure 2.2 compare powder and crack seizures made by the Drug Enforcement Administration (DEA) and the Federal Bureau of Investigation (FBI) in 1991 and recorded in the DEA's System to Retrieve Information from Drug Evidence (STRIDE). The charts compare seizures with respect to percentages meeting the criteria for 10-year, 5-year, and no (n/a) mandatory minimum sentences. Crack seizures are much more likely, under current mandatory minimums, to qualify for longer mandatory minimums. Since crack is more widely sold by African Americans, some civil rights advocates have sought to eliminate perceived bias against blacks in the current mandatory

---

[5]A case for such a distribution of sentences could be made on the grounds that the ultimate retail form of powder cocaine at higher levels is unknown. Thus, if crack is to be targeted for its dangerously addictive properties, it must be done at lower levels with consequently lower mandatory minimum triggers.

[6]Forst, 1995, p. 591, citing the *New York Times,* "U.S. Appeals a Case Defying Sentence Guides," August 29, 1993, p. 25.

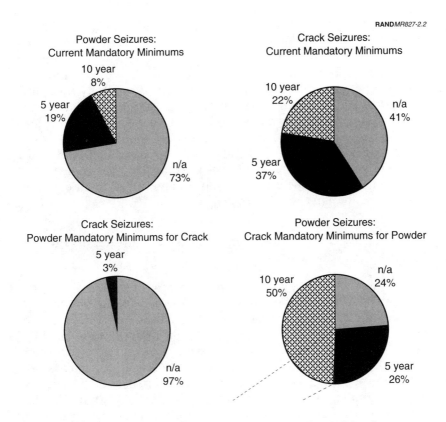

Figure 2.2—Comparison of Alternative Powder and Crack
Mandatory Minimums

minimums by eliminating the law's distinction between crack and
powder.[7] If this were done by using the present powder criteria for

_____

[7]On October 18, 1995, the House voted 332 to 83 against a U.S. Sentencing
Commission recommendation that would have brought crack cocaine trafficking and
possession in line with the lower penalties associated with powder cocaine. Later that
week, inmates at five federal prisons staged violent reactions to what they allegedly
saw as discrimination in sentencing (Associated Press, October 22, 1995). On October
30, 1995, President Clinton signed P.L. 104-38, which disapproved the U.S. Sentencing
Commission's recommendations, stating "the sentence imposed for trafficking in a
quantity of crack cocaine should generally exceed the sentence imposed for trafficking
in a like quantity of powder cocaine." A second attempt to bring sentences for crack
and powder into line has focused on raising sentences for powder.

crack, as well, and if seizure rates were unchanged from 1991, then the percentages triggering different levels of mandatory minimums would be as shown in the lower left pie chart in Figure 2.2. Under these assumptions, there would be a much greater difference between powder and crack than at present. Practically no crack seizures would trigger mandatory minimum sentences, compared with the quarter of powder seizures that would (upper left pie), assuming the current powder criteria continue. If, on the other hand, crack criteria were applied to powder, the results would be as shown on the lower right, for 1991 seizure rates. For consistency, this (two right-hand graphs) might be judged an improvement over the current situation (two upper graphs).

Determining Drug Amounts by Mixture Weight Versus Pure Weight

Drugs such as cocaine and heroin are commonly diluted, but the mandatory minimum sentences (and, for that matter, the federal sentencing guidelines) are based on the total weight of the mixture containing the substance in question, not the pure weight of the drug itself. Thus, for example, someone possessing 100 grams of a powder that is 10 percent pure heroin is subject to a five-year mandatory minimum at the federal level. Someone caught possessing 25 grams of pure heroin is not, even though this individual has two-and-a-half times as much heroin as the first one. This leads to some perverse effects. First of all, it reinforces the incentive for dealers to possess and sell drugs at a higher purity. Second, it means that punishment severity may principally reflect amounts of inactive ingredients or medium of distribution rather than amount of drug.

LSD further exemplifies the lack of relation between amount of pure drug and length of sentence. Sale of 10 grams of LSD-containing substance is punishable by a 10-year mandatory minimum sentence, and sale of 1 gram by a 1-year mandatory minimum, regardless of whether the substance is sugar, blotter paper, or liquid (i.e., pure LSD). But these media vary widely in LSD contained per gram (Scotkin, 1989). As shown in Figure 2.3, a dealer possessing a hundred 0.05-milligram doses of LSD would draw a 10-year minimum sentence if the LSD was in sugar cubes (total weight, 227 grams) and a 5-year mandatory minimum if it was on blotter paper (total weight,

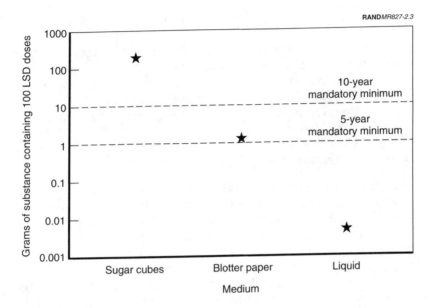

RAND*MR827-2.3*

Figure 2.3—Sentences Vary for Selling the Same Number of LSD Doses, Depending on the Medium Containing the Drug

1.4 grams). Selling the 100 doses in liquid form (total weight, 0.005 gram) would not trigger a mandatory minimum. But LSD in liquid form is, in some respects, the most dangerous because the desired doses are so small that it is difficult to control the amount ingested, which raises the likelihood of overdose.

The law is as stiff for coca leaves as it is for powder cocaine: the quantity-possessed triggers for mandatory minimums are the same. Yet, coca leaves are only about 2 percent cocaine. It is basically "safe" to ingest coca leaf; this has been practiced for over a thousand years and is not terribly addictive. Five hundred grams of leaf— enough to trigger a five-year federal mandatory—can produce between 1.5 and 2 grams of either powder cocaine or crack (Kennedy, Reuter, and Riley, 1994, pp. 46–47)—not enough of either to draw a five-year mandatory minimum on a first offense. Thus, although the law is tougher on crack than on powder, in some sense it is even tougher on leaf than on crack.

Shifting Power from Judges to Prosecutors

As indicated above, the authority once possessed by judges to decide on sentences within broad guidelines has, in the case of mandatory minimums, not been narrowed so much as it has been transferred to prosecutors. Though judges are required to impose specified sentences in certain situations, prosecutors are generally not required to charge a count carrying a mandatory minimum if other options are available. Prosecutors may use this flexibility as a bargaining chip in securing cooperation or a guilty plea for a lesser charge.

Is this transfer of authority wise? Judges, of course, tend to dislike mandatory minimums because they entail a loss of control over what has traditionally been their bailiwick and a loss of ability to implement an internally consistent sentencing policy (see the subsection above on eliminating disparity). It might further be argued that judges are empowered by the federal and state constitutions to play the role of judge. Perhaps that role should not be transferred to individuals who are selected differently and occupy a different place in the political structure. Public accountability might be curtailed by shifting more of the sentencing authority from public statements by a judge to private bargains between prosecutors and defense attorneys. However, the public has long perceived judges as perhaps too "soft" on criminals and may feel more comfortable with having discretion in the hands of "tougher" prosecutors. Subtler arguments based on roles and functions within the criminal-justice system may not carry much political weight.

Failing to Spare Unwitting or Peripheral Actors

As we have mentioned, mandatory minimums have been criticized for punishing the "little guy" while being more lenient on larger-scale dealers or "kingpins." Some people are getting long sentences for small amounts of crack, and, as discussed above, even large amounts do not necessarily imply the individual is a big dealer. Furthermore, in individual cases, the lack of discretion allowed to judges has dictated outcomes that appear unjust. Families Against Mandatory Minimums, an advocacy group, has cited cases of citizens who were otherwise apparently law-abiding and who did not wish to facilitate the drug trade; nonetheless, they wound up with long prison terms for their purportedly unwitting or peripheral involvement. Naturally, these are not typical cases, and they might still have been "oversentenced" in the absence of mandatory minimums. But the balance of justice in the United States has traditionally been weighted in favor of ensuring freedom for the innocent even if it means that some of the guilty are not punished. To some critics, mandatory minimums constitute a worrisome shift in this balance. On the other hand, according to Senator Orrin Hatch,

> of the 3,430 crack defendants convicted in 1994, the number of youthful, small-time crack offenders with no prior criminal history and no weapons involvement, sentenced in Federal courts, was just 51.... Only 10 percent of crack defendants had trafficked less than 2–3 grams of crack—the equivalent of 40–60 doses (Sen. Hatch, *Congressional Record*, S14307, September 26, 1995).

CONCLUSION

While the weight and force of arguments offered against mandatory minimums may seem impressive, it should be kept in mind that some of these allegations are hypothetical and have yet to be verified. Others might be addressed through amendments to current law that leave the basic concept of mandatory minimums intact. And in response to those that are verified and not addressed through amendment, it could be asserted that the gains from mandatory minimums are worth such costs. Although we cannot address all gains and costs, we can analyze some central, tangible ones. It is to that analysis that we now turn.

Chapter Three

COST-EFFECTIVENESS AT REDUCING COCAINE CONSUMPTION AND EXPENDITURES

In this chapter we present the approach we take and the results we obtain from our analysis of the cost-effectiveness of mandatory minimums and other control alternatives at reducing consumption of cocaine and expenditures on it. First, we come as close as we can to answering the general question: What if mandatory minimums were imposed on drug dealers meeting the specified quantity-possessed criterion in all jurisdictions in the United States? Because there are no national data on quantity possessed at time of arrest, we cannot answer that question directly, but we can say what happens when longer sentences are imposed on all convicted dealers.

Second, we seek to estimate the cost-effectiveness of applying federal mandatory minimums to those prosecuted at the federal level who meet the quantity-possessed criterion. Since such individuals are likely to be higher-level dealers than those prosecuted at state and local levels, mandatory minimums should impose higher costs and result in bigger market effects.

We answer those two questions in turn. For each, we describe the problem and the way we went about modeling it. We then present the cost-effectiveness results for extended sentences and for the benchmark alternatives—more conventional enforcement and treatment of heavy users. Finally, we see what happens to our results when we vary our assumptions.

This chapter is intended for the reader principally interested in our findings and the reasons behind them. Here we give only an outline of our methodology. Part II of this report gives details of the model-

141137

ing, data sources, and the more technical aspects of interpreting the results.

LONGER SENTENCES FOR ALL DRUG DEALERS

In this section, we analyze the cost-effectiveness of increasing the sentence length of drug dealers convicted in federal and state courts. Two programs previously analyzed by Rydell and Everingham (1994) provide benchmarks for assessing the performance of the longer-sentences program. Specifically, we estimate the benefits of spending an additional million dollars on each of the following:

- **Longer sentences:** increasing the sentences served by a representative set of drug dealers to 5 or 10 years (from the average term of 1 year served by dealers exiting prison in 1990).

- **Conventional enforcement:** further seizure of assets and products from drug dealers and arrest and incarceration of drug dealers at federal, state, and local levels, for terms equivalent to those served by prisoners exiting in 1990.

- **Treatment of heavy users:** offering additional amounts of the current mix of outpatient and residential treatment services to heavy cocaine users.

Note that we refer in this section to "longer sentences" instead of mandatory minimums. A mandatory minimum is not incurred unless some specified amount of cocaine can be associated with the convicted dealer's crime. Because state mandatory minimum laws vary widely and because our data at the state and local level pertain to all dealers and not just those meeting the triggering condition, we cannot assess the effects of mandatory minimums at the state and local level. However, we can learn useful lessons from a policy of extending sentences for a representative sample of *all* convicted dealers to lengths typical of federal mandatory minimums. This, of course, represents a very strict variant on the mandatory minimum concept, one in which any amount of drug is sufficient to trigger the mandatory sentence. In the next section, we show how targeting can increase the cost-effectiveness of long sentences and of enforcement in general.

In estimating how much a million dollars can buy, we account for expenditures for drug treatment, law enforcement personnel, and prison operation. Benefits are measured primarily by the reduction in cocaine consumption. However, the analysis also considers the effect programs have on numbers of users and on user expenditure for cocaine.

It may not be obvious how the three programs reduce cocaine consumption, so let us consider that briefly before proceeding. Longer sentences reduce consumption by increasing the amount of money charged by dealers to compensate them for the risk of additional prison time and of drug and other asset seizures.[1] These extra charges, in the form of cocaine price increases on the street, lead to decreases in consumption in two ways. They decrease current consumption by causing existing drug users to cut back the amount they buy, and they decrease future consumption by altering the flows of people into and out of drug use.

Conventional enforcement reduces consumption by seizing product, seizing assets, and arresting and incarcerating drug dealers.[2] All of these actions impose costs on drug dealers that cause additional price increases and, consequently, additional consumption decreases. Treatment of heavy users reduces consumption for two reasons: First, most users are off drugs while they are in a treatment program, and, second, some users stay off drugs after the treatment program is over.

---

[1]The increased risk might be high enough that some drug dealers would quit the market, so that enforcement would deter sales. However, the customers of these dealers would probably then be supplied by other dealers who are more tolerant of risk. Hence, we prefer a different formulation, in which all dealers have their price. This additional price, when passed on to consumers, will reduce consumption, thus providing a form of deterrence at that level. See also the discussion of deterrence in black markets in Chapter Two.

[2]As noted in Chapter One, "conventional enforcement," in this analysis, is enforcement of domestic laws against drug dealing. It does not include user sanctions or financial investigations of "money laundering." Nor does it include enforcement against dealers outside of the United states: controlling coca production and processing in source countries and interdicting shipments en route to U.S. wholesalers. See the end of this section for how the interdiction and source-country control programs compare to the longer-sentences program.

Modeling the Dynamics of Cocaine Control

Over the years a variety of models have been used to inform drug policy analysis. Many were essentially descriptive in nature (Schlenger, 1973; Leven, Roberts, and Hirsch, 1975; Gardiner and Schreckengost, 1987; and Homer, 1990, 1993a, b) or evaluated particular classes of interventions—e.g., interdiction—in isolation (Reuter and Kleiman, 1986; Cave and Reuter, 1988; Crawford and Reuter, 1988; Caulkins, 1990; Caulkins, Crawford, and Reuter, 1993; Kennedy, Reuter, and Riley, 1993; and Riley, 1993a, b). In 1990, RAND's Drug Policy Research Center (DPRC) began a concerted, long-term effort to build on this work and extend it into true policy simulation models that compare both supply- and demand-control programs on both cost and effectiveness dimensions.

The work began by updating and enhancing the descriptive models by developing spreadsheet-based "systems models" for cocaine, heroin, and marijuana (Childress, 1994a, b; and Dombey-Moore and Resetar, 1994). Such system models could track the production pipeline and highlight inconsistencies in quantity estimates. The next step was to incorporate these purely descriptive models into a prescriptive one that includes "policy levers" that allow estimation of how policy changes (e.g., changing the funding for an intervention) affect outcomes.

In moving toward a prescriptive model, work has focused to date on cocaine because in many respects it poses the greatest problems in the United States. The initial step was to build a model of cocaine user behavior that could trace the effect on consumption of changes in initiation and persistence of drug use (Everingham and Rydell, 1994). The cocaine-demand model specified stocks and annual flows between nonusers, light users (defined to be less than weekly users), and heavy users (at least weekly). (See Figure 3.1.) Surveys of drug use among household, homeless, and incarcerated populations were used to estimate flow rates in the base case. Analyses of enforcement and treatment programs included estimating how changes in program levels affect these flows. Enforcement (via price increases) decreases inflows to drug use and increases outflows from drug use, while treatment of heavy users increases the flows out of heavy use.

RAND*MR827-3.1*

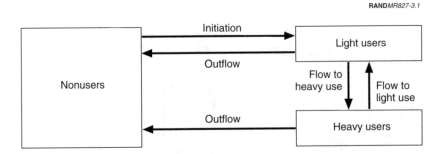

Figure 3.1—Annual Dynamics of Cocaine Use

The next step was to construct (Rydell and Everingham, 1994) a model of the cocaine market and how control programs affect supply, demand, and the market equilibrium price and level of cocaine consumption (see Figure 3.2). This model accounts for price effects both on the number of users and on consumption per user. Using newly available evidence we were able to improve upon several of the parameter estimates used in the Rydell and Everingham (1994) analysis. Notably, we have increased the estimate of the extent to which consumption responds to changes in price. (See Chapter Seven for updated parameter estimates and for conversion of incarceration data into costs and benefits.)

Reduction of Cocaine Consumption by Alternative Programs

Table 3.1 gives the model's principal output—the decrease in cocaine consumption resulting from a decision to spend one million 1992 dollars[3] on each of the three control programs. The rows in

---

[3]All cost calculations in this report are in 1992 dollars. The choice of a reference year for cost figures is arbitrary. We choose 1992 to facilitate comparison with the results of earlier analyses. To convert 1992 dollars into 1996 dollars (the latest year for which inflation data are available), multiply by 1.119. To convert benefits per million 1992 dollars to benefits per million 1996 dollars, divide by 1.119. Thus, 12.648 kilograms of cocaine consumption reduced per million 1992 dollars spent is 11.30 kilograms of cocaine consumption reduced per million 1996 dollars spent.

The number in Table 3.1 and elsewhere are displayed with far greater precision than is warranted by our data and methods. We display such precision to allow readers to follow our calculations with as little impediment as possible from round-off of inter-

RAND*MR827-3.2*

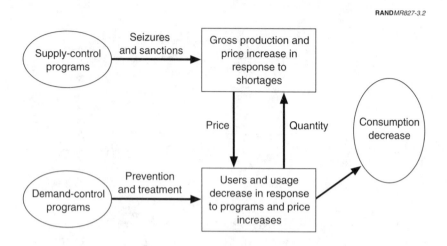

Figure 3.2—Structure of the Cocaine-Control Model

Table 3.1 give the year-by-year benefits of actions (treatment, en-forcement, or sentencing) taken in the first year that generate a stream of public costs[4] that amounts to an additional million dollars when discounted to present value.[5]

The table gives the benefits per million dollars spent treating heavy users (second column); expanding arrests, seizures, and incarcera-tion accomplished through additional conventional enforcement (third column); and extending sentences for convicted dealers (fourth column). In the case of the enforcement programs, these are

---

mediate results. Of course, the last digit must usually be rounded off, so the reader must occasionally make some allowance for slight divergence of the values presented from those he or she calculates.

[4]By "public costs" we mean costs to the public at large, i.e., to society, as opposed to costs to drug dealers. We do not restrict ourselves to costs to government. Enforcement costs are almost entirely government costs, but some treatment pro-grams are funded by the private sector.

[5]We follow the conventional assumption in economic analysis that people prefer spending a dollar now to spending it later (leaving aside the likelihood of inflation). Therefore, future dollars are discounted at an annual rate to make them comparable with current dollars.

Table 3.1

Cocaine Consumption Averted by Cohort Year of Alternative Million-Dollar Programs

	Kilograms of Consumption Averted Per Million Dollars Spent on Each Program		
Cohort Year	Treatment of Heavy Users	Conventional Enforcement	Longer Sentences
1	17.496	12.493	5.636
2	8.561	1.379	0.645
3	8.486	1.400	0.655
4	8.414	1.415	0.662
5	8.346	1.426	0.667
6	8.278	1.434	0.671
7	8.212	1.438	0.673
8	8.145	1.439	0.673
9	8.078	1.438	0.673
10	8.009	1.435	0.671
11	7.939	1.429	0.669
12	7.866	1.422	0.666
13	7.792	1.414	0.662
14	7.716	1.404	0.657
15	7.637	1.393	0.652
NPV, 4%	103.584	27.479	12.648

SOURCE: Runs of the revised cocaine-control model documented in Rydell and Everingham (1994), with a 15-year evaluation horizon, a $37,500 per person-year cost of incarceration to suppliers, a 12 percent dealer discount rate, and a –1.0 price elasticity of demand.

NOTE: NPV is net present value.

the benefits accruing from applying funds to additional action against a representative cross-section of dealers arrested at state and federal levels.

All three programs have their greatest effect in the first year. For the conventional-enforcement and longer-sentences programs, the first year is when the extra incarceration risk is driving up prices and thus driving down the quantity of cocaine demanded by current users. Since we are assessing the impact of a single year's program, after the first year there is no additional incarceration risk so prices and consumption levels per user return to roughly their previous levels. The small residual effect of the sanctions programs after year one is from year one changes in user flows (see Figure 3.1) that have long-term market effects.

The first year is also when users are being treated and when most are off cocaine during the three to four months (on average) that they are in treatment. After the first year, some people who receive treatment go back to heavy cocaine use, and some people who are no longer heavy users would have stopped heavy use even without treatment. The cocaine-control model takes account of these events and estimates the net reductions in cocaine consumption caused by the treatment program over time.

The last row in Table 3.1 (presented graphically in Figure 3.3) shows that the longer sentences are not cost-effective relative to the benchmark alternatives. Per million program dollars, imposing longer sentences reduces consumption only half as much as conventional enforcement, and only one-eighth as much as treatment of heavy users.

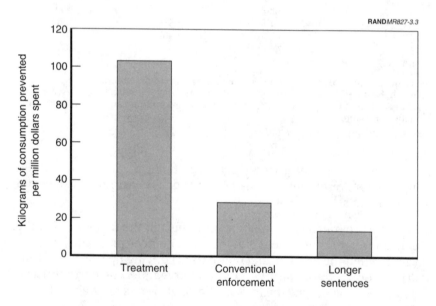

Figure 3.3—Cocaine Consumption Prevented Per Million Program
Dollars Spent at Federal, State, and Local Levels

Conventional enforcement is a mixture of seizures (of product and assets) and imprisonment (of drug dealers). Analyzing its cost-effectiveness relative to that of mandatory minimums yields an important lesson: The imprisonment part of the mix is the less cost-effective part, so that adding to it yields marginal cost-effectiveness that is below the conventional-enforcement average. Moreover, due to dealer discounting of future imprisonment costs, the incarceration-years added by longer sentences affect the price of cocaine less than do the incarceration-years caused by conventional enforcement.

Effect of Evaluation Horizon and Supplier Cost of Incarceration

The finding that the longer-sentences program is less cost-effective than alternative programs depends upon the evaluation horizon used in the analysis, and on the decision to evaluate the program's performance when targeted on the average convicted cocaine dealer. Decreasing the evaluation horizon, or targeting the program on higher-level dealers (who require higher-risk premiums), would increase the relative cost-effectiveness of the longer-sentences program. However, as the following threshold analyses show, one has to move a considerable distance in these directions to change the program rankings reported in Table 3.1 and Figure 3.3.

Evaluation Horizon. The above cost-effectiveness results assume that programs are evaluated over a 15-year period. Political considerations sometimes encourage shorter evaluation horizons. To show the effect that truncating the evaluation horizon can have, Figure 3.4 varies that horizon from 1 to 15 years. For each year of the period analyzed, we show the present value of costs and benefits through that year, disregarding all later costs and benefits and expressing the result as kilograms of reduction in consumption per million program dollars.[6]

---

[6]The values for a 15-year evaluation period (on the right border of Figure 3.4) are the same as the last row in Table 3.1.

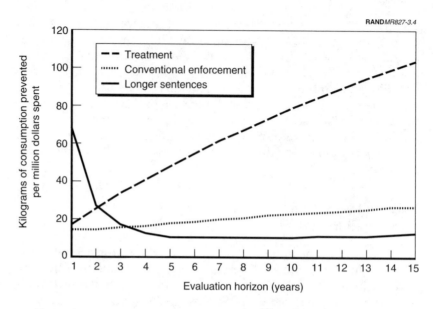

**Figure 3.4—Consumption Reduction Per Million Program Dollars by
Alternative Evaluation Horizons**

The conventional-enforcement program has almost all its public
costs but only half its benefits (costs imposed on suppliers) in the
first two years. So the longer the evaluation horizon the greater the
recognized benefits are per dollar of recognized cost. In other words,
the line for this program in Figure 3.4 increases as the evaluation
horizon lengthens, because an increasing amount of benefits is
counted against the costs incurred in the early years.

This effect is even more noticeable in the case of the treatment
program. Treatment costs occur immediately (treatment rarely lasts
longer than a year), but the benefits of drug-free user years
accumulate over many years. So, the treatment-program line in
Figure 3.4 climbs markedly as the evaluation horizon lengthens and
more and more benefits offset the program's cost, which occurred
entirely in the first year.

For mandatory minimums, in contrast, the public costs of the
additional prison spaces do not peak until five years in the future. In

the case of an individual, for example, who would have been in prison anyway for the average one-year sentence, no extra cost at all accrues from the application of mandatory minimums until the second year. However, the supplier costs generated by longer sentences occur immediately. As ex-plained above, the reason why increased prison sentences have an immediate effect on supplier cost is that drug dealers require additional compensation for the increased risk of incarceration. Thus, the consumption decreases caused by this program occur largely before the public costs must be paid. Accordingly, the shorter the evaluation horizon, the better longer sentences will look relative to treatment.

Just how myopic a perspective is necessary for longer sentences to appear cost-effective? If the evaluation period is less than 3-1/3 years, then longer sentences seem more cost-effective than conventional enforcement. If the evaluation period is less than 2 years, then longer sentences are more cost-effective than treatment. Beyond these thresholds (and certainly by 15 years, as we have already seen) longer sentences are less cost-effective than either of the other two alternatives. Thus, someone would have to be interested only in short-term costs and consequences if longer sentences are to look cost-effective relative to the alternatives.

Supplier Cost of Incarceration. The drug-dealer convictions produced by conventional enforcement yield a range of types of dealers to whom sentences can be given. Under our assumption of a representative mix, the cost to suppliers of an additional person-year of incarceration equals the amount of compensation the average dealer requires to offset the risk of a year in prison. Our analysis assumes this average risk premium to be $37,500 per year (in 1992 dollars).

However, if longer sentences were targeted on higher-level dealers, the risk premium would be larger, which means that the cost to suppliers of a given number of additional person-years of incarceration would be higher. The result would be greater cost-effectiveness for the longer-sentence program, because cost imposed on suppliers would be higher while the cost to the public for the program would be unchanged.

Figure 3.5 shows the effect of varying the supplier cost of incarceration for the additional person-years of incarceration caused by the longer-sentences program from $0 to $350,000. Note that the supplier cost of incarceration is being varied only for the longer-sentences program, because that is where the targeting occurs. The supplier cost of incarceration for conventional enforcement remains the same, because that program's incarceration of the average convicted drug dealer is unchanged.

Over the range of risk premiums explored, the cost-effectiveness of the longer-sentences program varies from 0 to 118 kilograms of cocaine consumption prevented per million dollars spent on additional sentence length (see the bold line in Figure 3.5). The longer-sentences program becomes more cost-effective than conventional enforcement if the cost to suppliers (for the additional sentence

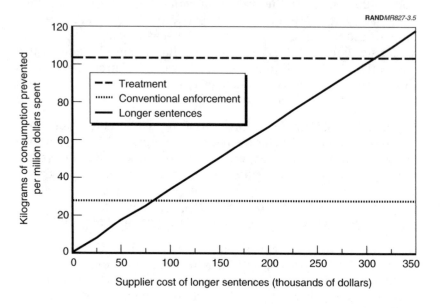

Figure 3.5—Consumption Reduction Per Million Dollars by Alternative
Supplier Costs of Longer Sentences

duration) is over $75,000 per person-year of incarceration.[7] It be-
comes more cost-effective than treatment of heavy users if the cost
to suppliers is over $300,000 per person-year of incarceration.

Sensitivity to Uncertain Parameters

The results in Table 3.1 and Figure 3.3 depend on a set of assumptions about cocaine dealers and consumers. Reliable data on dealer
and consumer behavior are scarce enough that no analysis of the cocaine market can be complete without an examination of the sensitivity of the results to variations in the assumptions.

What happens if dealers and consumers do not behave as we have
assumed they would? In the previous subsection we showed what
happens to the results when we vary the supplier costs of longer sentences by targeting the program to higher-level suppliers. But there
is a distinct issue arising not from enforcement targeting but from
dealer motivation: The dealer cost we assume for the untargeted
program graphed in Figure 3.3 may not be the $37,500 we have as-
sumed. How much might it vary from that number? Certainly, the
plausible range of average values for an untargeted program is much
narrower than the range of all potential targeted programs that is
shown along the horizontal axis in Figure 3.5. Here, we examine how
varying dealer cost of imprisonment between $25,000 and $50,000 a
year influences the cost-effectiveness of all three programs, other
things equal.

There is also uncertainty about the appropriate annual discount rate
to use when computing the present value of that supplier cost. The
analysis above uses a 12 percent dealer discount rate. In this sensitivity analysis we vary this rate from a low of 4 percent (the same as
the assumed inflation-adjusted social discount rate) to a high of 20
percent. Finally, even with the newly available evidence, there re-

---

[7]This analysis is intended only to show the effects of a varying incarceration cost to
suppliers. It understates the incarceration cost at which longer sentences become
more cost-effective than conventional enforcement. The reason is that we do not vary
the value of drug and other asset seizures, which we would expect to be greater for
higher-level dealers. Those costs to dealers would increase only under additional conventional enforcement, not under longer sentences, where no additional arrests are
made. A full analysis of targeting is given in the next section.

mains uncertainty about cocaine's price elasticity of demand. Our current analysis uses –1.0 for this elasticity. In this sensitivity analysis we vary it from –0.5 to –1.5.

Table 3.2 reports the results of the sensitivity analysis. The first row gives the base-case parameter estimates and repeats the base-case results already seen in Table 3.1. Then, the following row pairs show the effect of varying each parameter over the indicated range. The values printed in bold type are those being varied. In each row pair, the low and high parameter values are considered in the order that increases the cost-effectiveness of longer sentences.

In all cases, varying the uncertain parameters over these ranges does not change the cost-effectiveness ranking of the alternative programs. Per million dollars spent on the program, longer sentences always achieve less consumption reduction than conventional enforcement, which in turn achieves less consumption reduction than treatment.

The bottom two rows of the table (presented graphically in Figure 3.6) show what happens if these parameters all take on their end-of-range values simultaneously. The first set of extreme parameter values favors the alternatives to longer sentences (i.e., they make the alternative programs look better relative to longer sentences). The second favors longer sentences (i.e., the parameter values make longer sentences look better relative to the alternative programs).

Neither of these sets of extreme parameter values is likely to be correct. The ranges examined for all these parameters are wide, and for the extreme values to occur at all is unlikely, let alone to simultaneously occur in a direction that either favors treatment or favors longer sentences. The point, however, is that the program ranking in these simultaneous-extreme cases is the same as in the base case. This analysis thus provides strong evidence that our conclusions about relative cost-effectiveness are robust in the face of uncertainty about these parameters.

Alternative Evaluation Criteria

As mentioned earlier, we are interested in benefit measures other than reduction in cocaine consumption. Does the order of prefer-

Table 3.2

Effect of Alternative Parameter Estimates on Consumption Results

Assumptions	Parameter Estimates			Kilograms of Consumption Averted Per Million Dollars Spent on Each Program		
	Price Elasticity of Demand	Supplier Cost of Incapacitation ($ per person-year)	Dealer Discount Rate (%)	Treatment of Heavy Users	Conventional Enforcement	Longer Sentences
Base-case analysis						
Base-case estimates	−1.0	37,500	12	103.6	27.5	12.6
Sensitivity to price elasticity of demand for cocaine						
Low elasticity	**−0.5**	37,500	12	88.0	11.7	5.3
High elasticity	**−1.5**	37,500	12	124.7	50.3	23.2
Sensitivity to supplier cost of incarceration						
Low supplier cost	−1.0	**25,000**	12	102.7	26.9	8.7
High supplier cost	−1.0	**50,000**	12	104.3	28.0	16.4
Sensitivity to annual dealer discount rate						
High dealer discount	−1.0	37,500	**20**	103.5	27.4	10.4
Low dealer discount	−1.0	37,500	**4**	103.7	27.6	16.0
Sensitivity to extreme combinations of parameters						
Favoring alternative programs	**−0.5**	**25,000**	**20**	87.7	11.5	3.0
Favoring longer sentences	**−1.5**	**50,000**	**4**	127.3	51.9	38.8

SOURCE: Runs of the revised cocaine-control model documented in Rydell and Everingham (1994).

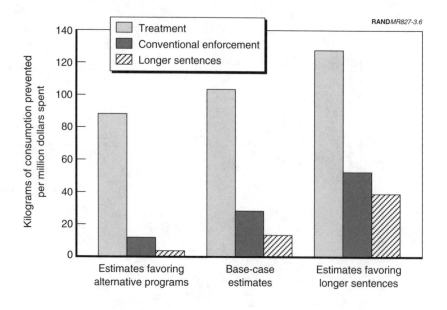

**Figure 3.6—Effect of Extreme Parameter Values: Estimates Favoring
Alternative Programs and Estimates Favoring Longer Sentences**

ence for programs change with the benefit measure? We answer this
question for crime and other social effects in Chapter Four. Here, we
examine some measures more directly related to market function.

User expenditures are important because not all of the problems associated with cocaine are a function of cocaine use by itself.
Certainly lost productivity and overdose deaths are directly caused
by cocaine use. But much of the market-related violence depends
more directly on the dollar value of the cocaine market than on the
quantity sold. Likewise, property crime committed to finance cocaine consumption probably depends more on how much users
spend than on how much they use.[8] Another way of measuring cocaine's toll is by estimating the number of users, or, taking time into

----

[8]In Chapter Four we will translate changes in cocaine consumption and spending into
other measures of interest, such as levels of crime.

account, user-years. We estimate both user-years and, because cocaine takes its greatest toll on heavy users, heavy-user-years.[9]

We find that the program rankings are similar for the various benefit measures (see Table 3.3). Per million dollars, longer sentences reduce consumption, user-years, and heavy-user-years less than conventional enforcement, and both enforcement approaches reduce them less than treatment.

On the user expenditure criterion, however, conventional enforcement is, marginally, the least successful. Treatment decreases user expenditures, while the enforcement programs have essentially no effect. The reason for that lack of effect is that these programs affect consumption through price increases. In this analysis we estimate that a 1 percent increase in price causes a 1 percent decrease in consumption, so expenditure (price times consumption) essentially does not change.

Table 3.3

Comparing Programs According to Alternative Evaluation Criteria

Outcome	Changes in Outcome Per Million Dollars Spent on Each Program		
	Treatment of Heavy Users	Conventional Enforcement	Longer Sentences
Cocaine consumption (kilograms)	–103.6	–27.5	–12.6
User expenditure on cocaine ($ million)	–8.64	0.20	0.12
Number of cocaine user-years	–586	–253	–118
Number of heavy-cocaine-user-years	–587	–81	–38

SOURCE: Runs of the revised cocaine-control model documented in Rydell and Everingham (1994).

---

[9]One user-year accumulates for every person who is in the user pool for one year; two user-years accumulate if a person stays two years in the user pool or if two people stay one year each; and so on. Heavy-user-years accumulate analogously with respect to the heavy-user pool.

Comparison with Additional Programs

The analysis above has focused on comparing the cost-effectiveness of longer sentences for drug dealers with two benchmarks: conventional enforcement and treatment. We found that the longer-sentences program is less cost-effective than either of those programs. However, the cocaine-control model enables comparison with two additional programs: interdiction of cocaine supply before it reaches the United States and control of cocaine supply in source countries. Rydell and Everingham (1994) found that both interdiction and source-country control were also less cost-effective than conventional enforcement (which they call domestic enforcement). The remaining question is, Are these additional programs more or less cost-effective than the longer-sentences program analyzed in our current report?

Updating the analysis in Rydell and Everingham (1994) to reflect revised parameter estimates (notably, the revised estimate of the price elasticity of demand for cocaine) produces the estimates in the second and fourth data columns of Table 3.4. Comparing these results with those already obtained (first and third data columns) shows that, on all cost-effectiveness measures, the longer-sentences program lies between interdiction and source-country control.

The results for the first evaluation criterion—consumption reduction—are presented graphically in Figure 3.7 for the enforcement alternatives. The ranking of the three alternatives to longer sentences is the same as in Rydell and Everingham (1994). The longer-sentences program ranks lower than interdiction but higher than source-country control.

MANDATORY MINIMUMS FOR FEDERALLY PROSECUTED DEALERS

One of the strengths of the dynamic model used above is that it takes into account the entire cocaine market and user population. Everything is considered. At the same time, in a sense, everything has to be considered; the model cannot meaningfully focus on segments of the market, and that is a limitation. For instance, using that model, we found that widespread use of longer sentences was not cost-effective. However, that does not say that mandatory mini-

Table 3.4

Comparing with Cost-Effectiveness of Other Enforcement Programs

	Changes in Outcome Per Million Dollars Spent on Each Program			
Outcome	Conventional Enforcement	Interdiction	Longer Sentences	Source-Country Control
Cocaine consumption (kilograms)	−27.5	−20.4	−12.6	−9.8
User expenditure on cocaine ($ million)	0.20	0.20	0.12	0.09
Number of cocaine user-years	−253	−191	−118	−21
Number of heavy-cocaine-user-years	−81	−61	−38	−29

SOURCE: Runs of the revised cocaine-control model documented in Rydell and Everingham (1994).

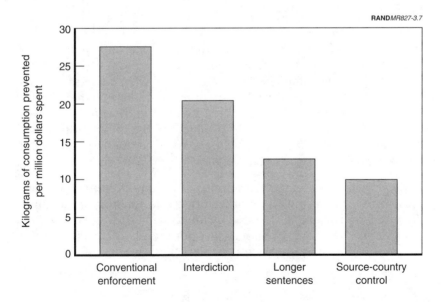

Figure 3.7—Comparison of the Longer-Sentences Program
with Other Enforcement Programs

mums are not appropriate for higher-level defendants, e.g., defendants who are prosecuted at the federal level and who are arrested in possession of quantities of cocaine sufficient to trigger a mandatory minimum sentence.

In this section we describe a new cost-effectiveness model. We apply it to federal-level defendants,[10] i.e., primarily cases investigated by the DEA and FBI, but also those of other federal agencies and the larger state and local cases that are prosecuted at the federal level. Although the model is more flexible (in that it is able to focus on particular types of dealers) and more detailed, it is static and, thus, cannot analyze the time horizon effects discovered with the previous model. Again, we compare imposing mandatory minimum sentences with devoting additional resources to traditional enforcement and sentencing. We will again include, as a foil, treating heavy users.

Modeling Strategy

We use a two-stage model that links programmatic spending to cocaine consumption and users' spending on cocaine. The first stage relates spending on an intervention to the products of that intervention. (See the upper portion of Figure 3.8.) For example, how many more drug dealers could be incarcerated and what value of their financial assets could be seized by spending another million dollars at the federal level on traditional enforcement and sentencing? We then translate the many diverse products of the interventions into two summary effects on the cocaine market: reduction in demand and costs imposed on drug suppliers.

In the model's second stage, a simple market equilibrium model calculates the impact on the market price and quantity of cocaine. Spending on cocaine is obtained by multiplying quantity consumed by price paid per unit. (See the lower portion of Figure 3.8. For details of the modeling approach, see Chapter Seven.)

---

[10]The identification of federal-level defendants with higher-level defendants can only be approximate. Recall from Chapter Two that high-level dealers are not always caught in connection with large drug seizures, so the larger seizures associated with federal-level prosecutions are not always indicative of higher-level defendants.

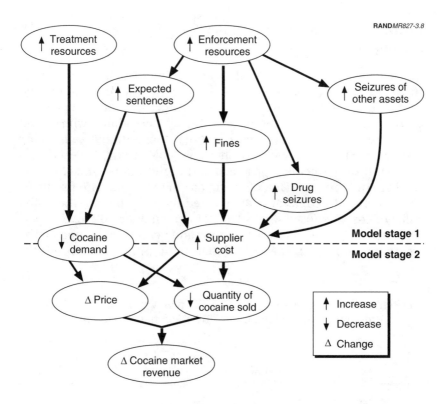

RAND*MR827-3.8*

**Figure 3.8—Static Model of the Consequences and Costs
of Controlling Cocaine**

In the remainder of this section we present our estimates of the cost-effectiveness of each of the three programs—more conventional enforcement at the federal level, extending federal-level sentences to mandatory minimum levels, and more treatment of heavy users. We do this first for a set of assumptions regarding model parameters—arrest costs, discount rate, etc.—that represent our best estimates of those parameters. We then vary these values in a set of sensitivity analyses to determine the extent to which our conclusions depend on our assumptions. Finally, we report briefly some additional cost-effectiveness analyses that exhibit the model's flexibility as an analytic tool and permit the inference of a rule of thumb for determining cost-effectiveness in this context.

Cost-Effectiveness Results Under "Best-Estimate" Assumptions

Table 3.5 summarizes the results of spending $1 million on each of three programs: (1) expanding conventional arrest, prosecution, and sentencing of federal-level offenders; (2) prosecuting under mandatory minimum laws some federal drug defendants who would otherwise have been prosecuted under conventional sentencing laws; and (3) treating heavy users. The table shows, for each program, both intermediate products and the ultimate impact on the market equilibrium. The following are the intermediate products: the number of people directly affected by the program, the dollar value of costs imposed on dealers per person affected (i.e., per person arrested for the first two programs and per person treated for the treatment program), the total dollar value of costs imposed, the

Table 3.5

Effects of Spending an Additional $1 Million on Various Cocaine Control Programs at the Federal Level: "Best-Estimate" Assumptions

	Program		
Outcome	Conventional Enforcement	Mandatory Minimums	Treating Heavy Users
Intermediate Effects			
Net govt. cost per person affected	$37,944	$68,785	$1,740
People affected	26.35	14.54	574.71
Cost imposed on dealers per person affected	$166,755	$168,822	$0
Total costs imposed	$4.39M	$2.45M	$0
Demand averted per person affected	0.332 heavy-user-years	0.605 heavy-user-years	1.112 heavy-user-years
Demand averted	8.74 heavy-user-years	8.80 heavy-user-years	638.80 heavy-user-years
Market Outcomes			
Change in consumption (Q)	–63.3 kgs	–36.0 kgs	–103.6 kgs
Change in market price (P)	$0.0276/gram	$0.0155/gram	$0.0123/gram
Change in spending (PQ)	–$134,400	–$135,100	–$9,815,800

number of heavy-user-years averted per person affected, and the total number of heavy-user-years averted. These effects are then translated into impacts on cocaine consumption (Q), price (P), and spending (PQ), using the market component of the model described above.

In terms of ability to reduce cocaine consumption, conventional enforcement is almost twice as cost-effective as mandatory minimums. As is apparent from the intermediate effects, mandatory minimums cost the government more per person affected. Thus, a million dollars does not go as far. While barely 15 additional persons can be made subject to mandatory minimums for a million dollars, 26 additional individuals can be arrested, prosecuted, and sentenced for an additional million dollars of conventional enforcement.[11] As a result, even though mandatory minimums impose about the same cost per person affected,[12] conventional enforcement imposes a higher total cost. For the two enforcement alternatives, it is these total costs imposed on the cocaine market that are chiefly responsible for the difference in reduction of cocaine consumption. An additional, though much smaller, effect is the decrease in consumption realized because some dealers are also cocaine users and it is much more difficult for them to consume while they are in prison. Overall, treatment is estimated to be about three times as effective as spending money to extend federal sentences from their current length to those under mandatory minimum sentencing.[13]

While mandatory minimums are less cost-effective than the alternatives, their disadvantage is less for this population of federal offend-

---

[11]Both the 15 and the 26 refer to additional arrests meeting the amount-possessed criterion for triggering mandatory minimums. Some of those individuals will not be successfully prosecuted. To compare the two programs fairly at the individual level, they must be denominated in like terms, e.g., dollars per arrestee, even though none of the million dollars for mandatory minimums is spent on arrests. See the beginning of Chapter Seven.

[12]That is, for each person arrested under a mandatory minimum regime, the *additional* prison time expected imposes a cost about the same as the costs that incarceration and asset forfeitures would be expected to impose on a person arrested under conventional enforcement.

[13]While we take into account, here and in the previous analysis, the direct reduction in demand brought about by incarcerating cocaine-consuming dealers, we do not account for reduction of supply through treatment of such dealers. Thus, we underestimate (if only to a small degree) the cost-effectiveness of treatment.

ers than for all offenders (see Figure 3.9). Federal mandatory minimums have 57 percent of the effect of additional conventional enforcement at the federal level. Recall that in the previous section, longer sentences were less than half as cost-effective as conventional enforcement ("typical dealers" bars in Figure 3.9). The better performance of mandatory minimums here reflects, for one thing, the greater value that the higher-level dealers targeted by federal programs place on their time.[14]   Again, treatment of heavy users was estimated to be eight times as cost-effective as longer sentences for typical dealers, compared to three times for the federal offenders analyzed here.

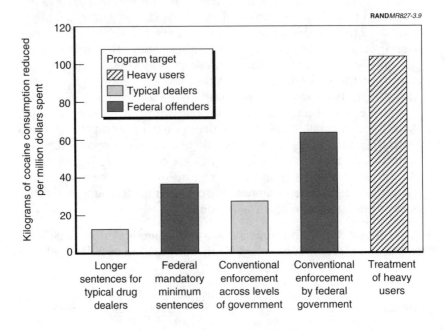

Figure 3.9—Benefits of Alternative Cocaine Control Strategies

---

[14]Figure 3.8 shows that federal mandatory minimums are more cost-effective than conventional enforcement against typical drug dealers. This supports a case for better targeting, not longer sentences. For a discussion of the relative cost-effectiveness of federal and lower-level enforcement, see Chapter Five.

In terms of reducing the dollar value of the cocaine market, mandatory minimums and conventional enforcement are about equally effective, but that effect is small—about 13.5 cents per dollar spent. Treatment is estimated to be over 70 times as effective as either enforcement approach. The gross difference between treatment and the supply control programs has a simple explanation. High-level enforcement reduces consumption by driving up price. Because users are estimated to decrease their consumption by 1 percent for every 1 percent increase in price (elasticity of demand = –1), the reduction in consumption is exactly as great as the increase in price (on a percentage basis) so there is no net effect on spending. The only way the enforcement programs reduce spending on cocaine is by incapacitating dealers who are also users and, thereby, reducing demand for cocaine. Not surprisingly, that is a very expensive way to reduce cocaine spending.

There are two principal conclusions from these results. First, where the enforcement programs are concerned, the greater the reliance on long sentences, the less cost-effective the program is at reducing cocaine consumption. Spending additional money on arrest, prosecution, and conventional sentencing is more cost-effective than spending additional money to extend terms served by *already arrested* federal defendants from the conventional average of 27 months to mandatory minimum levels averaging 80 months. (For derivation of sentence-length averages, see Chapter Six.)

Second, treatment is more cost-effective than either enforcement approach at reducing both cocaine consumption and cocaine spending. Treatment is solidly but not exceptionally more cost-effective than the federal-level enforcement programs at reducing consumption; it has a 1.6:1 edge over conventional enforcement and close to a 3:1 advantage over mandatory minimums. Treatment is enormously more cost-effective (on the order of 70 times more cost-effective) at reducing spending on cocaine.

Sensitivity Analyses

It is important to assess the extent to which these two principal conclusions are sensitive to the input values used in the model. The goal of this section is to perform such sensitivity analyses relative to the consumption results (one excursion for the revenue results is given in Chapter Seven). These analyses also generate insight into why the results turn out the way they do and intuition about related policy questions. We begin by varying the values we assume for our inputs one at a time, then show the implications for our results when we vary inputs more than one at a time.

Single-Variable Sensitivity Analyses. The first step is to report the effect of varying each input variable in turn over a range that is at least as broad as what subjectively seems plausible. As Table 3.5 shows, the model generates a large number of outputs, and it would be more confusing than instructive to list the impact of every input change on every output. Instead we focus on two key ratios that bear directly on the two principal conclusions drawn above: (1) the ratio of the cost-effectiveness of treatment to the cost-effectiveness of extending sentences to match mandatory minimum sentences and (2) the corresponding ratio for conventional enforcement and extending sentences, both in terms of ability to reduce cocaine consumption. In the base case for reducing cocaine consumption, these ratios are 2.9:1 and 1.8:1, respectively. Given these two ratios, we also know the relative cost-effectiveness of treating heavy users and federal-level enforcement with conventional sentencing; it is simply the ratio of these two ratios.

Table 3.6 reports the sensitivities of the cost-effectiveness ratios to changes in the input values from the "best estimates," or base-case values, underlying the results in Table 3.5. Again, this is cost-effectiveness at reducing cocaine consumption. The table does not cover every input variable, but the others

- are known fairly precisely (e.g., the cost to the government of in-carcerating someone for one year),

- have minimal impact (e.g., the expected magnitude of any fine paid by convicted dealers or the probability that a dealer was a light drug user), or

- have effects deducible from the results given. For example, a change in the adjudication cost per arrest has the same effect as an identical change in the arrest cost itself.

Variations in four of the nine variables shown in Table 3.6 do not have much effect on the cost-effectiveness of mandatory minimums

Table 3.6

How Between-Program Ratios for Cost-Effectiveness at Reducing Cocaine Consumption Vary with Input Variable Values

Input Variable	Values	Cost-Effectiveness Relative to That of Mandatory Minimums for Federal Defendants	
		Treatment	Federal-Level Conventional Enforcement
Elasticity of demand	−1 (base value)	2.9	1.8
	−0.5	5.5	1.7
	−1.5	1.9	1.8
Cost imposed on dealers per year in prison	$85,000 (base value)	2.9	1.8
	$37,500	6.2	2.5
	$130,000	1.9	1.5
Police cost per arrest	$20,000 (base value)	2.9	1.8
	$10,000	2.9	2.4
	$30,000	2.9	1.4
Fraction of dealers who are heavy users	23.5% (base value)	2.9	1.8
	0%	3.0	1.8
	47%	2.8	1.7
Rate at which dealers discount future events	0.12 (base value)	2.9	1.8
	0.04	2.1	1.4
	0.06	2.3	1.4
	0.18	3.6	2.1
	0.30	5.4	3.0
Value of drugs seized per arrest	$48,646 (base value)	2.9	1.8
	$25,000	2.9	1.5
	$100,000	2.9	2.3
Value of other assets forfeited per arrest	$15,000 (base value)	2.9	1.8
	$7,500	2.9	1.4
	$30,000	2.9	3.2
Average sentence with mandatory minimum	80 months (base value)	2.9	1.8
	60 months	2.7	1.7
	120 months	3.2	2.0
Fraction of arrests leading to trial for mandatory min. sentence	30% (base value)	2.9	1.8
	17%	2.9	1.7
	60%	2.9	1.8

relative to the other alternatives. Variations in three of the others affect the cost-effectiveness of mandatory minimums relative to conventional enforcement.

- If dealers discount future events at less than 12 percent per year, they perceive the costs of a longer prison sentence as greater. A cut to 6 percent or 4 percent reduces conventional enforcement's cost-effectiveness advantage from 80 percent to 40 percent. Again, the reason lies in the greater perceived costs of longer sentences when the future is not discounted as much.

- Increasing the costs of arrest by 50 percent also cuts conventional enforcement's advantage in half, making the extension of sentences for the already-arrested look less unattractive than it did.

- In the event we have overestimated the nondrug assets forfeited per arrest, say by 100 percent, conventional enforcement's advantage over mandatory minimums is also reduced by half. A 50 percent underestimate, on the other hand, almost triples conventional enforcement's advantage over mandatory minimums—and gives it an advantage over treatment. The great sensitivity of conventional enforcement's margin to this parameter is because it is the only one of the three alternative that brings about increased asset forfeitures. Forfeiting assets reduces the net cost to the government of making an arrest, and, of course, it increases dealers' cost of selling drugs.

Two other variations affect the cost-effectiveness of mandatory minimums relative to treatment:

- If the cost imposed on dealers is $130,000 instead of $85,000 per year in prison, imprisonment is much better at driving up supply costs and so reducing cocaine consumption. As a result, treatment's cost-effectiveness advantage over mandatory minimums drops from 2.9:1 to below 2:1.

- If cocaine buyers are much more responsive to price changes than we assume, mandatory minimums gain in cost-effectiveness relative to treatment. Greater responsiveness (elasticity) means greater changes in consumption for a given expenditure on either enforcement or treatment, but the effect on consumption in the case of enforcement is more direct.

The important point to take away from Table 3.6, though, is that none of the substantial changes in input variables considered made mandatory minimums as cost-effective as conventional enforcement. Neither did any changes leave treatment with much less than a 2:1 advantage in cost-effectiveness over mandatory minimums. Some other changes, generally no more improbable than those discussed above, resulted in cost-effectiveness advantages of 4:1 or more for treatment and 2.5:1 or more for conventional enforcement, relative to mandatory minimums.

Multiple-Variable Sensitivity Analysis. As discussed above, the most consequential input choices include those for the elasticity of demand, the cost imposed on dealers per additional year of imprisonment, and the cost to police of making an arrest. To understand better the sensitivity of the results to these key variables, we want to examine how the results change when more than one of the inputs is varied simultaneously.

We do so for two variables at a time by means of a graph known as a strategy region graph. The graph shows the combinations of input values for which a particular policy is most cost-effective. In the analyses illustrated below, one of the inputs varied is cost imposed on dealers per year of imprisonment (on the vertical axis). The other variables are, in Figure 3.10, arrest cost, and, in Figures 3.11, 3.12, and 3.13, elasticity of demand, with arrest cost varying from one figure to the next. (Other inputs, including those listed in Table 3.6, are held constant as these are varied.)

These graphs include stars indicating the values assumed for the base case. Note that in every case the star lies comfortably within the region where treatment is the most cost-effective way to spend a marginal million dollars. Thus, the chief conclusions are not very sensitive to combinations of two inputs being varied simultaneously. However, we discuss the implications of wide variations in the inputs to determine whether there are any useful lessons to be drawn for extreme cases.

Among the most interesting of the extreme cases is depicted in Figure 3.10. If the value of a drug dealer's time is high enough (i.e., if

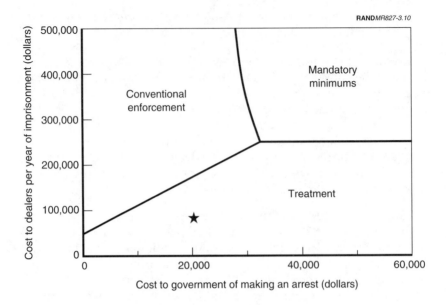

**Figure 3.10—Combinations of Arrest and Dealer Imprisonment Cost
Values Leading to a Cost-Effectiveness Advantage
for Different Programs**

the dealer is at a very high level), then spending more money on enforcement will become cost-effective. How high is high enough? With the base case input values, if the cost imposed on dealers per additional year of imprisonment rose from $85,000 per year to about $175,000 per year, then conventional federal-level enforcement would be as effective as treating heavy users at reducing U.S. cocaine consumption. Naturally, as the arrest cost increases, the cost-effectiveness of conventional enforcement drops and dealers must be at even higher levels (reflected in higher costs imposed per year of imprisonment) if enforcement is to be preferable to treatment. If the arrest cost rises high enough, there is a shift in the most economical form of enforcement. Specifically, if the arrest cost rises above $30,000, the number of additional drug dealers arrested per million dollars falls so much that greater total costs can be imposed through spending the million dollars on extending sentences to mandatory minimum levels. Thus, if all other variables are at base-case levels, mandatory minimum sentences are the most cost-effective only if two conditions pertain. First, the cost imposed on dealers per year of imprisonment must be at least $250,000 per year. Second, the dealers must be unusually difficult to catch, with average arrest costs over $30,000.[15]

Considering the annual dollar profits of a wholesale dealer helps put the $250,000-per-cell-year figure in perspective. Suppose a mid-level wholesale dealer buys shipments of 10 kilograms of cocaine for $150,000 and sells the cocaine a kilogram at a time for $25,000 per kilogram,[16] yielding revenues of $10,000 per kilogram sold. The dollar profit per kilogram is thus $10,000 minus whatever the dealer pays for workers and materials. Thus, individuals for whom the cost of imprisonment is more than $250,000 per cell year must be at least at the level of wholesale dealers who sell 25 kilograms per year. Indeed, they must really be still higher than that because the dollar profit per kilogram must be reduced to cover the dealer's risk of death or injury and the amount he or she would demand as compensation for imprisonment.

The other three graphs examine the responsiveness to elasticity of demand and costs imposed by prison, given different costs to the government of making an arrest. In Figure 3.11, we again see that by tracing upward from the star, enforcement becomes more cost-effective than treatment at an annual dealer cost of imprisonment of roughly $175,000, with other inputs at base-case values. However, the lower the elasticity of demand (in absolute value), the higher must be the cost imposed by imprisonment if enforcement is to be

---

[15]By using average sentences and costs of imprisonment to dealers, we omit detail that is more likely to work in favor of conventional sentences than mandatory minimums. If we had distributions of these values, we could determine the outcome if judges successfully matched the longest sentences to the defendants associated with the highest incarceration risk premiums, for both enforcement approaches. We suspect that the potential difference between maximum and average sentences is greater for conventional sentences than for mandatory minimums.

[16]The $150,000 and $25,000 figures are consistent with the loglinear price model developed by Caulkins and Padman (1993) and Caulkins (1994) when the gram-level price is $129.20/pure gram (as is assumed here), the wholesale purity is 86.8 percent (typical of wholesale purities recorded in STRIDE), and the quantity discount factor is 0.778, which is typical of the values Caulkins (1994) observed for cocaine.

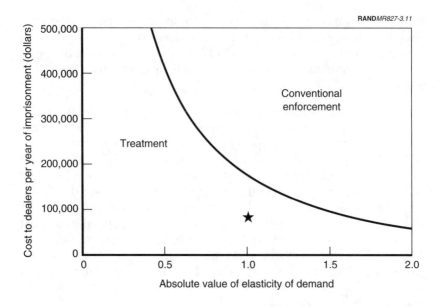

Figure 3.11—Combinations of Elasticity and Dealer Imprisonment Cost Values Leading to a Cost-Effectiveness Advantage for Different Programs (Arrest Cost = $20,000)

preferable to treatment. The reason is that at lower elasticities, consumption is less responsive to enforcement-induced increases in price. As the arrest cost increases to $30,000 (Figure 3.12), the threshold for enforcement cost-effectiveness increases to about $240,000. Much above this amount, at about $340,000, mandatory minimums become the most cost-effective alternative. At an arrest cost of $40,000 (Figure 3.13), mandatory minimums are the more cost-effective enforcement alternative over a wide range of elasticities.

Finally, we varied the values of eight inputs (including those graphed here) simultaneously over ranges resembling those given in Table 3.6. This was done by assuming a distribution for each variable and drawing values at random, then repeating this over a large number of trials (16,000). Although the results varied appreciably from those for "best-estimate" assumptions in many of the trials, in only a handful of cases were mandatory minimums more cost-effective than either

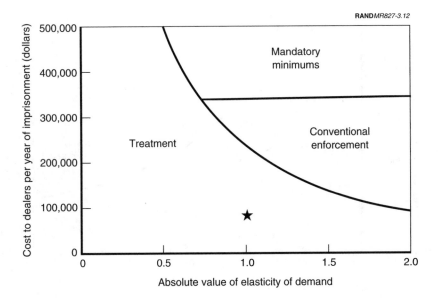

RAND*MR827-3.12*

Figure 3.12—Combinations of Elasticity and Dealer Imprisonment
Cost Values Leading to a Cost-Effectiveness Advantage for
Different Programs (Arrest Cost = $30,000)

of the other alternatives. (For a full discussion of this analysis, see
the end of Chapter Seven.)

Other Findings: Low-Level Offenders, Seizures

The analyses relating to high-level offenders suggest that street-level
enforcement that leads to prison terms for low-level offenders will
not impose enough costs on dealers to be cost-effective. To what extent is this true? The model can readily be adapted to answer such
questions. Suppose, for example, the government were to spend $1
million arresting, prosecuting, and incarcerating for 90 days street-
level dealers with these characteristics: value of time = $25,000 per
year, easier to catch (average arrest cost = $2,000 plus an adjudica-
tion cost of $1,300 per arrest), possess about one-half ounce of co-
caine (worth $750), have no seizable assets, and fail to pay any fine.
How many kilograms of cocaine consumption could that be ex-

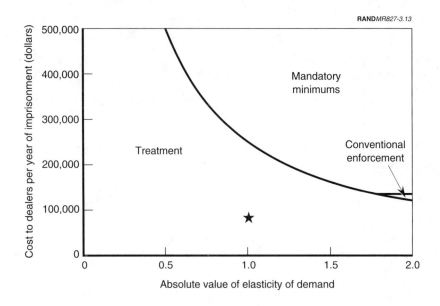

Figure 3.13—Combinations of Elasticity and Dealer Imprisonment
Cost Values Leading to a Cost-Effectiveness Advantage for
Different Programs (Arrest Cost = $40,000)

pected to avert through the mechanism of imposing costs on dealers
that are passed along to users?

The model suggests that, on average, each such arrest would cost the
government $8,367 for incarceration and other costs, impose costs
on drug dealers of $4,881, and avert about one-twentieth of a heavy-
user-year of consumption. Thus, each million dollars spent would
avert about 9.1 kilograms of cocaine consumption. That is about
one-seventh what would be achieved spending $1 million on high-
level conventional drug enforcement.

An important caveat to this result is that street-level enforcement can
have other effects besides imposing costs on dealers. For example, it
can abate nuisance aspects of drug markets and increase search time
(nondollar) costs for users. Hence, this calculation does not imply
that high-level enforcement is better than street-level enforcement,
but rather implies that *if* street level enforcement is effective, it is not

solely because of its ability to impose costs on dealers in the sense modeled here.

The model can also inform us about other approaches to enforcement. Suppose one had the opportunity to seize one kilogram of cocaine whose value and hence replacement cost was $21,500. Suppose further that there was no chance of making an arrest and, therefore, no chance of incurring any costs of prosecution, seizing any assets, putting someone in prison, etc. The only immediate consequence is the seizure of a kilogram of cocaine. What is the most one could spend making that seizure and still be as cost-effective as conventional federal enforcement at reducing cocaine use? The model indicates the answer is about $6,300. To be as effective as treating heavy users? About $3,000. Consider seizing one metric ton of cocaine valued at $10,000 per kilogram, again with no chance of making any arrests. Parallel calculations suggest one could spend $2.9 million making the seizure and still be as cost-effective as conventional federal enforcement or $1.4 million and still be as cost-effective as treatment.

More generally, in terms of reducing cocaine use, enforcement programs are as cost-effective as treating heavy cocaine users if they impose costs on dealers of at least $7.20 for every taxpayer dollar spent on the program. In terms of reducing spending on cocaine, enforcement programs must impose costs on dealers of at least $38.20 for every taxpayer dollar spent if they are to be as cost-effective as treatment.

These ratios allow one to develop simple rules of thumb. For example, when would extending the sentence of a drug dealer do more to reduce cocaine use than spending the same number of dollars on drug treatment? Since it costs about $25,000 per year to keep someone in federal prison, the answer is whenever the cost to the dealer of being in prison is at least $7.2 \times \$25,000 = \$180,000$.

If we could apply the same test to arresting persons possessing varying amounts of cocaine, we could determine the minimum amount for which incarceration would be a cost-effective response. However, such a test cannot be applied to possession. Sometimes low-level couriers with a low value of avoiding prison are asked to carry large quantities; conversely, very high-level dealers who are willing and able to pay large sums to avoid prison often take precautions to never be physically in possession of the drugs they control. Hence, other factors besides amount possessed, such as evidence about the defendant's role in the drug distribution system, must be considered in determining whether meting out long sentences is going to meet the test of being a cost-effective way to reduce cocaine use.

CONCLUSION

The principal results derived from analyses of typical and federal defendants are that (1) conventional enforcement is more cost-effective than extending sentences and (2) treatment is more cost-effective than enforcement. Both of these apply whether the goal is to reduce cocaine use or spending on cocaine. The sensitivity analyses show that, when we vary substantially the values we assume for inputs such as elasticity, arrest cost, cost imposed on dealers by imprisonment, and dealer discount rate, the principal results just stated do not change. The sensitivity analyses do show, however, that, for some combinations of input values, federal mandatory minimum sentences can be more cost-effective than the other interventions. It is not plausible that these combinations could pertain to the average federal mandatory minimum defendant, but there may be individuals who meet these criteria.

Chapter Four

OTHER MEASURES OF COST-EFFECTIVENESS

In Chapter Three, we analyzed the cost-effectiveness of mandatory minimum sentences relative to both conventional enforcement and treating heavy users. We defined cost-effectiveness in two ways: (1) ability to reduce cocaine consumption per million taxpayer dollars spent on the program and (2) ability to reduce drug users' spending on cocaine per million taxpayer dollars spent.

Those are two key evaluation metrics, but clearly there are other relevant outcomes. In this chapter, we discuss how these alternative programs might compare on other dimensions. The analyses underlying these discussions range from informed opinion to elementary algebraic estimates. The goal is not to be highly precise, but rather to give a feeling for some of the considerations excluded above. As it turns out, none of these considerations threaten to overthrow the basic conclusion that enforcement with conventional sentencing is more cost-effective than enforcement with mandatory minimum sentences. Nor do they challenge our conclusion that treatment is more cost-effective at controlling cocaine than is mandatory minimum sentencing.

ABILITY TO REDUCE USE OF OTHER DRUGS

The analyses above focused on the ability of the modeled programs to reduce cocaine consumption and spending on cocaine, but they can also affect consumption of other drugs, legal and illegal. When enforcement reduces consumption by driving up cocaine prices, the user may not be quitting all drugs but substituting others such as amphetamines, heroin, or alcohol. In contrast, because some users consume more than one drug and most treatment is not drug-specific, treating cocaine use would tend to reduce consumption of other drugs.

It is not possible to be more precise because little is known about the cross-elasticities of demand for different drugs, i.e., the percentage change in consumption of one drug that occurs when the price of another increases by 1 percent. Anecdotal evidence of substitution has existed for some time (e.g., Rottenberg, 1968). With one exception, however, formal studies have addressed only substitution between marijuana and alcohol (McGlothlin, Jamison, and Rosenblatt 1970; Model, 1992; DiNardo and Lemieux, 1992). In the one exception, Model (1993) studied the impact of marijuana decriminalization on emergency room mentions not only for marijuana but also for other drugs.[1] Mentions for marijuana went up and those for other drugs went down, suggesting that marijuana is a substitute for other drugs.

To the extent that such substitution exists or that treating polydrug users for cocaine use reduces their consumption of other drugs, the results in Chapter Three understate the effectiveness of treatment relative to that of the enforcement programs.

ABILITY TO CONTROL CRIME

The nexus between drugs and crime has been studied extensively. (See, e.g., Dembo, 1994). The analysis here is quite rudimentary by comparison. We make no attempt to model or capture ways in which this relationship varies or could vary over time, over birth cohorts, or across ethnic groups. The goal is only to describe the relationship, not to explain it—and not, for that matter, to describe it very precisely.

Our analysis is based on Goldstein's (1985) tri-partite framework for categorizing drug-related violence into (a) psychopharmacological, (b) economic-compulsive, and (c) systemic crime. We generalize this concept to all drug-related crime (not just violent crime).

---

[1]As reported by the Drug Abuse Warning Network, about which see Caulkins, Ebener, and McCaffrey (1995). An "emergency room mention" refers to identification of a drug in the system of a person admitted to a hospital through an emergency room.

Psychopharmacological crime occurs because "some individuals, as a result of short- or long-term ingestion of specific substances, may become excitable, irrational, and may exhibit violent behavior" (p. 494). Psychopharmacological violence may involve drug use by either the offender (e.g., irritability associated with withdrawal from heroin leading to spousal or child abuse) or the victim (e.g., severely intoxicated individuals may be inviting targets for robbery). Since it is a function of drug use, we assume it to be proportional to the quantity of drugs consumed.

Economic-compulsive crime occurs when drug users commit felonies such as robbery or burglary to support their habit. The principle motivation of the perpetrator is economic gain, so much of this crime is nonviolent, e.g., theft and prostitution. Sometimes, however, acquisitive crime can turn violent, as with robbery or instances in which a burglar is surprised by a homeowner and a fight ensues.

Systemic crime is the type of crime discussed in Chapter Three as contributing to drug supply costs (in proportion to the value of drugs sold) because it takes the place of a judicial system as a means of resolving disputes. Systemic crime "refers to the traditionally aggressive patterns of interaction within the system of drug distribution and use" (Goldstein, 1985, p. 497). Goldstein's examples include disputes over territory between rival dealers, robberies of dealers and retaliation for such robberies, disputes over the quality of drugs sold, punishment for failure to pay a debt, and violence used to enforce normative codes (e.g., punishment for abusing another dealer's "brand name"). Since economic-compulsive and systemic crime are market-related forms of crime, we assume they are proportional to drug spending.

In Chapter Three, we estimated how spending $1 million on each of three programs (conventional sentencing, mandatory minimum sentencing, and treating heavy cocaine users) would affect cocaine consumption and spending on cocaine. We now make the simplifying assumptions that changes in psychopharmacological crime are proportional to changes in consumption, and that changes in both economic-compulsive and systemic crime are proportional to changes in cocaine spending. Thus we need to estimate just three "proportionality constants" that convert changes in consumption and spending into changes in levels of different types of crime. (We extend the analysis from Chapter Three on federal defendants rather than that on all defendants because enforcement was found relatively more cost-effective in the former.)

The methodology employed for estimating these constants (detailed in Appendix D) is transparent. We (1) estimate the current amount of drug-related crime, (2) estimate the fraction of that crime that is related to cocaine, and (3) divide by the current amount of consumption or spending to find the average amount of crime per unit of spending or consumption.

The limitations of this methodology are also transparent. There are no good estimates of the amount of drug-related crime. We do not know for certain how to apportion amounts of drug-related crime across drugs. And there is no reason to believe that the marginal rate associated with spending an additional million dollars would equal the average rates we calculate here. Finally, the marginal rate might vary with the nature of the program that brought about the change in spending or consumption. For example, if greater street enforcement led to lower spending on drugs, drug-market-related violence might still go up if that street enforcement led to greater disorder in the drug markets; i.e., the average level of violence might increase as the market gets smaller, but only for conventional enforcement. Nevertheless, since the goal is only to create rough, plausible estimates, this procedure is adequate.

Table 4.1 shows the "proportionality constants," or changes in the number of crimes per unit change in consumption and spending on cocaine, that are derived in Appendix D. Note that there is much more economic-compulsive and systemic crime than there is psychopharmacological crime. Enforcement might also prevent some nondrug crime by incarcerating people (e.g., domestic violence perpetrated by the high-level drug dealers); that possibility is not addressed here.

Table 4.2 applies these "proportionality constants" to the base-case model results from the federal-level analysis in Chapter Three. The relative impact of the three policies on the various crimes is generally similar (e.g., small reductions in homicides, big reductions in assaults), so it is useful to have an aggregate measure of the amount of

Table 4.1

Crime Associated with Cocaine Consumption and Spending

	Psychopharmacological Crimes Per Metric Ton	Economic-Compulsive Crimes Per Billion $	Systemic Crimes Per Billion $	Economic-Compulsive Plus Systemic Crimes Per Billion $
Homicide	3	19	95	110
Sexual assault	24			
Agg. assault	480	1,800	7,400	9,200
Simple assault	700	3,400	14,000	17,000
Robbery		7,300		7,300
Burglary		28,000		28,000
Larceny		120,000		120,000
Auto theft		2,700		2,700

Table 4.2

Change in Number of Crimes, Per Million Program Dollars Spent: Federal-Level Enforcement Versus Treatment

	Conventional Enforcement	Mandatory Minimums	Treating Heavy Users
Personal crimes			
Homicide	−0.21	−0.13	−1.4
Sexual assault	−1.5	−0.9	−2.5
Robbery	−1.0	−1.0	−72.0
Agg. assault	−31.4	−18.4	−139.8
Simple assault	−46.7	−27.6	−239.5
Property crimes			
Burglary	−3.8	−3.8	−279.5
Larceny	−16.3	−16.4	−1,193.2
Auto theft	−0.4	−0.4	-26.8
Total serious crime	−36	−23	−383

crime averted.   One such measure is the number of so-called "serious" crimes. Following Greenwood et al. (1994), we use crimes designated as "serious" under California law. These crimes include murders, rapes, aggravated assaults, robberies, and burglaries of residences. Thus, to estimate impact on serious crime, we add together the first four rows of Table 4.2 and 60 percent of the sixth row (since residential burglaries make up about 60 percent of all burglaries). The results are shown in the last row.

We find no difference between conventional enforcement and mandatory minimums in relation to property crime; the former, however, should reduce crimes against persons by about 70 percent more than the latter. But treatment should reduce serious crimes (against persons as well as property) the most per million dollars spent—on the order of 10 to 15 times as much as would the incarceration alternatives.

What are the reasons behind these results? Most drug-related crime is economically motivated—undertaken, e.g., to procure money to support a habit or to settle scores between rival dealers. Fewer crimes are the direct result of drug consumption—crimes "under the influence." However, since we found very little difference between conventional enforcement and mandatory minimums in their effects on the money flowing through the market, we thus see very little difference in their effects on economically motivated crime. On the other hand, since we found appreciable differences in consumption effects, we see appreciable differences in effects on crimes "under the influence." The latter are more likely than are economically motivated crimes to be crimes against persons.

But treatment has an enormous advantage over enforcement in reducing the economic value of the cocaine market—larger even than that found in Chapter Three for reducing cocaine consumption. Why is that? When a treated offender stays off drugs, that means less money flowing into the market. But when a dealer facing the risk of a longer sentence raises his price, say 1 percent, to compensate, buyers will reduce the amount of cocaine they purchase. The best evidence suggests that reduction will be something on the order of 1 percent. Thus, the total revenue flowing through the cocaine market stays about the same, and so do the incentives for economically motivated drug-related crimes. Therefore, the effect of the enforcement alternatives is limited almost entirely to the relatively small number of crimes "under the influence." Treatment, however, has an advantage against those crimes similar to the advantage shown in Figure 3.9 (relative to the dark bars) and an even greater advantage against the larger number of economically motivated crimes.

Table 4.2 suggests that treatment is far and away more cost-effective at reducing serious drug-related crime than are the enforcement interventions, even when restricted to federal-level offenders. Whereas treatment was 2 to 3 times as cost-effective in terms of reducing co-caine use, it is estimated to be 10 to 15 times more cost-effective at reducing serious crime. The reason is that treatment is much more effective at reducing *spending* on cocaine, and much drug-related crime is driven by spending on cocaine (that which is economic-compulsive or systemic), not use per se (as is psychopharmacological crime).

Table 4.3 parallels Table 3.6. It examines the sensitivity of treat-ment's crime-reduction advantage to variation in the values we assume for inputs to the model. In particular, it examines the relative ability to reduce serious and violent crime of (1) treatment versus extending sentences and (2) conventional enforcement versus extending sentences. In the base case these ratios are 16.9:1 and 1.6:1, respectively.

The table shows that the conclusions about ability to reduce crime are robust with respect to variation in the input values. However, there are two kinds of uncertainty here. The first is our uncertainty about the influence of our assumed input variables on the model's estimate of changes in cocaine use and spending, which is reflected in the table's results. The second is that concerning the modeling of the connection between drug use and spending and drug-related crime. The second is the larger, so the estimates of the impact on crime are much less precise than is suggested by the simple sensitiv-ity analysis shown in Table 4.3. (For a sensitivity analysis varying eight inputs simultaneously, see the end of Chapter Seven.)

IMPACT ON SOCIAL COSTS

In some sense, one would like to reduce all outcomes of each inter-vention to a single denominator (e.g., dollars), calculate the net benefits in terms of that denominator, and be able to unambiguously state exactly how cost-effective each intervention is. That is not possible, but we can take modest steps in that direction. There are two dominant categories of social costs, drug-related crime and health effects associated with drug use. Suppose we assumed the former can be proxied by the number of serious drug-related crimes, and the latter is proportional to the quantity consumed. Then the

Table 4.3

Sensitivity of Conclusions About Crime-Reducing Effectiveness with Respect to Variation in Assumptions

Input Variable	Values	Cost-Effectiveness Relative to That of Mandatory Minimums for Federal Defendants	
		Treatment	Federal-Level Conventional Enforcement
Elasticity of	−1 (base value)	16.9	1.6
demand	−0.5	NA[a]	NA
	−1.5	3.6	1.8
Cost imposed on dealers	$85,000 (base value)	16.9	1.6
per year in prison	$37,500	29.6	2.0
	$130,000	12.0	1.5
Police cost per arrest	$10,000 (base value)	16.9	1.6
	$3,000	16.9	2.2
	$30,000	16.9	1.3
α = Fraction of	0.55 (base value)	16.9	1.6
selling costs proportional	0.25 (β=0.35; γ=0.4)	9.6	1.7
to quantity	0.85 (β=0.05; γ=0.1)	22.7	1.5
β = Fraction of	0.20 (base value)	16.9	1.6
selling costs proportional	0.05 (α=0.625; γ=0.325)	18.2	1.6
to enforcement	0.35 (α=0.475; γ=0.175)	15.5	1.6
γ = Fraction of	0.25 (base value)	16.9	1.6
selling costs proportional	0.05 (α=0.65; β=0.3)	19.3	1.6
to value of market	0.45 (α=0.45; β=0.1)	14.3	1.6
Fraction of	23.5% (base value)	16.9	1.6
dealers who are	0%	21.1	1.8
heavy users	47%	14.1	1.5
Rate at which	0.12 (base value)	16.9	1.6
dealers discount	0.04	13.1	1.3
future events	0.06	14.0	1.4
	0.18	20.1	1.8
	0.30	26.9	2.3

Table 4.3—continued

| Input Variable | Values | Cost-Effectiveness Relative to That of Mandatory Minimums for Federal Defendants | |
		Treatment	Federal-Level Conventional Enforcement
Value of drugs seized per arrest	$17,700 (base value)	16.9	1.6
	$5,000	16.9	1.4
	$50,000	16.9	2.0
Value of other assets seized per arrest	$10,000 (base value)	16.9	1.6
	$4,000	16.9	1.3
	$25,000	16.9	2.9
Average sentence with mandatory minimum	84 months (base value)	16.9	1.6
	60 months	16.0	1.5
	120 months	18.7	1.8
Fraction of arrests leading to trial for mand. min. sent.	30% (base value)	16.9	1.6
	17%	16.8	1.6
	50%	17.3	1.6

[a]If the elasticity of demand is less than about 0.83 (in absolute value), then the enforcement programs would actually increase, not decrease the amount of serious and violent crime. The reason is that when the elasticity of demand is less than 1 (in absolute value), driving up the price of cocaine increases total spending on cocaine, which would tend to increase economic-compulsive and systemic cocaine-related crime, even as the amount of psychopharmacological cocaine-related crime decreased.

relative ability of our three programs to reduce social costs would be a linear combination of the relative abilities to reduce serious crime and to reduce consumption, two things we have already estimated. That is to say, the relative ability to reduce social costs would be intermediate to these two previously calculated relative abilities.

To be more specific, we know from Chapter Three that treatment is about three times as cost-effective at reducing cocaine use than is extending the sentences of federal-level offenders eligible for mandatory minimum sentences. (Again, we extend the federal-level analysis to give enforcement the benefit of the doubt.) Likewise, we know from the previous subsection that in terms of ability to reduce serious crime, this ratio increases to about 17 times. Hence, treatment is between 3 and 17 times as effective at reducing total social costs as is mandatory minimum sentencing.[2] The exact ratio depends, for example, on the importance one attaches to reducing crime relative to reducing drug-related adverse health consequences. There is no correct or "objective" answer to how one should trade off reductions in crime with reductions in harms related to drug use. Table 4.4 gives one example of how a health-related social cost might be attached to a kilogram of cocaine consumed. It is based on Rydell and Everingham's (1994, pp. 38 and 77) interpretation of social cost estimates from Rice et al. (1990) and Fisher, Chestnut, and Violette (1989), adjusted for inflation. It suggests a figure on the order of $31,000 per kilogram consumed (subject to all of the strengths and limitations of the original estimates of social costs).

Finding a basis for estimating the social cost per serious and violent crime is also difficult. Cohen (1994) and Cohen, Miller, and Rossman (1994) have published estimates of the tangible and intangible costs

Table 4.4

Some Social Costs of Cocaine Abuse in the United States
(in 1992 dollars)

Item	Effect
Hospital stay ($ millions/yr)	716
Morbidity ($ millions/yr)	3,179
Mortality ($ millions/yr)	5,044
Total cost ($ millions/yr)	8,939
Consumption (metric tons/yr)	291
Unit cost ($ thousands/kg)	31

SOURCE: Rydell and Everingham (1994, pp. 38 and 77), drawing from social costs given primarily by Rice et al. (1990) and Fisher, Chestnut, and Violette (1989).

---

[2]Assuming that all cocaine-related social costs depend either on the amount consumed or the revenue generated in the cocaine market (or both).

of various types of crime. These numbers are far from universally accepted; Zimring and Hawkins (1995) criticize the whole concept of trying to attach dollar figures to intangible costs such as pain and suffering. But if one applies these numbers to the mix of crimes averted by the three programs considered here, one obtains composite numbers on the order of $8,000–$9,000 in tangible (economic) costs per serious crime and $23,000–$31,000 in intangible costs. The total would thus be about $31,000–$40,000 per serious crime.

Another way to think about the value of averting a serious crime is from the perspective of opportunity cost: How much would one be willing to spend on some other approach to avert such a crime? Greenwood et al. (1994) estimate that, if fully implemented, California's "Three Strikes and You're Out" law will cost California taxpayers about $16,000 per serious crime averted. They also estimate that more efficient versions of laws that enhance sentences for repeat offenders might bring this figure down to about $12,000 per serious crime.

But as mentioned above, these approaches to estimating social costs are marked by a great deal of subjectivity. Figure 4.1 can help the reader assess the implications of judgments of social costs. Find on the horizontal axis a subjective valuation of social cost that should be associated with a serious drug-related crime.[3] Likewise, on the vertical axis an estimate can be chosen (e.g., by varying the numbers in Table 4.4) of the average health-related social costs avoided per kilogram reduction in cocaine consumption. The corresponding point on the chart indicates the estimate of how much more cost-effective treatment is at reducing social costs than is extending sentences for drug offenders. That is, if the point lies near the "T = 7.5M" line, then the consequence of the cost choice is that treatment would be about seven and a half times more effective than mandatory minimums at averting social costs.

---

[3]Roughly speaking, for every 200 serious drug-related crimes, there is one murder and fewer than 10 rapes; the rest of the offenses are assaults, burglaries, or robberies. When considering the enforcement-oriented interventions, most of the other crimes that would be averted would be assaults. With treatment, most of these other crimes averted would be property crimes.

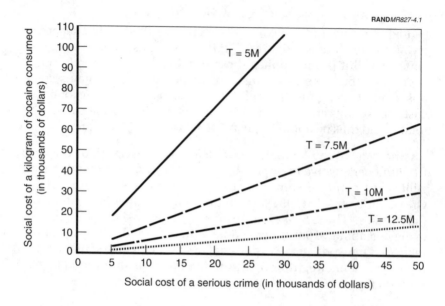

Figure 4.1—How Assumed Social Costs Influence Relative
Cost-Effectiveness of Treatment (T) and Extending
Sentences (M)

Chapter Five

CONCLUDING OBSERVATIONS

PROGRAM EFFECTIVENESS

The preceding chapters included some rather detailed and, in places, complicated analyses, so it is worth pausing to discuss their implications. The first conclusion deriving from the analysis is that extending sentences for all drug dealers is less cost-effective than expanding the scope of conventional enforcement by arresting and prosecuting more dealers under traditional sentencing laws. Thus, if the objective is to increase the stringency of drug enforcement in a manner that maximizes the benefits obtained per dollar spent, expanding conventional-enforcement budgets is preferable to passing laws increasing sentence length.

Why is conventional enforcement more cost-effective than longer sentences such as those imposed by mandatory minimums? The analysis shows that drug enforcement can usefully be thought of as comprising two components, each of which is costly for taxpayers and each of which contributes to keeping drugs expensive: (1) arrest and conviction, which impose costs on suppliers principally through the seizure of drugs and other assets and (2) incarceration of convicted defendants. The fact that arrest and conviction impose costs on dealers is sometimes overlooked amid complaints about the "revolving door" of justice. However, it turns out that, on average, arrest and conviction impose greater costs on dealers per taxpayer dollar spent than does incarcerating dealers. Since extending sentences amounts to altering the mix of these two components of enforcement in favor of incarceration, it dilutes or reduces the efficiency of enforcement relative to simply expanding both components proportionately.

Longer sentences, however, can be more efficient if they are limited to drug dealers with a higher-than-average position in the distribution hierarchy. This sort of targeting is achieved to some degree by mandatory minimums. For a mandatory minimum sentence to take effect, certain conditions must be met, e.g., some threshold quantity of drugs has to have been in the convicted person's possession at the time of arrest. Federal law regarding mandatory minimum drug sentences contains such quantity triggers, along with other provisions regarding prior convictions. Furthermore, we assume that dealers prosecuted at the federal level are more likely to be at mid to upper levels of the distribution hierarchy than are those prosecuted at lower levels of government.

Our second conclusion, however, is that even the level of targeting achieved by mandatory minimum sentencing is not enough to make such sentences more cost-effective than conventional enforcement against similar offenders.

A third conclusion, though, is that there does exist a class of drug dealers for whom long sentences such as those imposed by federal mandatory minimums are more cost-effective than conventional enforcement. That class is identified by two distinguishing characteristics. First, they must be substantially more difficult to arrest than the typical dealer apprehended by federal agencies. Second, they must demand very high compensation for the risk of spending a year in prison, on the order of the annual dollar profits of someone who makes 25 one-kilogram cocaine sales per year. A typical drug dealing hierarchy might have retail sellers buying fractions of an ounce to re-sell in fractions of a gram, first-level wholesale dealers buying multiple ounces to resell as fractions of an ounce, second-level wholesale dealers buying kilograms to resell in multiple ounce lots, and third-level wholesale dealers selling kilograms at a time. This suggests that sentences as long as federal mandatory minimums might be cost-effective for some third-level wholesale dealers, but not for their subordinates.

Since there are many different state-level mandatory minimum drug sentencing laws, it is possible that some achieve a degree of targeting sufficient to make the laws cost-effective at reducing drug use. This report does not undertake a state-by-state examination of state-level mandatory minimum sentencing laws but does provide guidelines that can be used to make such judgments.

Our fourth conclusion is that the targeting principle applies across types of enforcement. Not only are long sentences for dealers qualifying for federal mandatory minimums more cost-effective than long sentences for typical dealers, but conventional enforcement directed against dealers qualifying for federal mandatory minimums is more cost-effective than conventional enforcement applied to typical dealers.

Because federal enforcement is more targeted at higher-level dealers than are state and local efforts, state and local enforcement is typically less cost-effective at driving up drug prices than are federal efforts. However, local enforcement is more directly able to respond to the problems generated by street markets, ranging from simple disorder to drive-by shootings. Hence, one might infer that local enforcement should be freed, to some extent, from the expectation or obligation that it must seek to impose costs on dealers generally. Instead, it should be allowed to focus on dealers who generate problems beyond those inherent to selling—problems such as violence and the exploitation of youths for criminal labor.

A fifth conclusion is that treatment is more cost-effective at controlling drug use, drug spending, and drug-related crime than is either conventional enforcement or long sentences, whether targeted through mandatory minimum "trigger" provisions or applied generally. The parts of that conclusion relating to drug use and spending are not new; earlier work already found that treatment was more cost-effective than domestic enforcement at controlling cocaine use and users' spending on cocaine. Our current work simply updates that conclusion by incorporating newer estimates of how responsive consumption is to changes in drug prices and refines it by breaking down domestic enforcement generally into some of its constituent parts.

The part of this conclusion pertaining to drug-related crime is new. Treatment has a substantial advantage over controlling drug-related crime because most drug-related crime is motivated not (directly) by drug use but rather by drug spending. Drug dollars motivate users to commit property crimes to finance their habits and dealers to fight over drug market revenues. And treatment has a big advantage over enforcement in reducing drug spending. The reason is that spending is the product of consumption and price. Enforcement results in a drop in consumption but a rise in price, while treatment directly reduces the demand for drugs but has little effect on their price. Thus, treatment has a greater effect on spending.

Our sixth conclusion is that mandatory minimum sentences should seem most appealing to people with very short time horizons. The benefits of imposing mandatory minimum sentences are realized up front, whereas the costs come due in the future. In contrast, the costs and benefits of conventional enforcement are roughly contemporaneous, and with treatment the costs come early and the benefits accrue over time. Thus, mandatory minimums are analogous to financing purchases with a credit card, conventional enforcement to paying cash, and treatment to investing. Mandatory minimums might be supported by people with no concern for cost and benefits accruing more than a few years in the future, even though such sentences are not cost-effective for society as a whole.

POLICY IMPLICATIONS

The conclusions drawn about effectiveness above are of general interest with regard to debating and formulating drug policy. However, this report was motivated by a rather specific policy question: Are mandatory minimum drug sentences a good policy that should be extended or should they be repealed? There is no one answer to that question. Different people will have different opinions depending on their values and what they think drug control policy should strive to achieve. Some might support mandatory minimums because they think such sentences constitute "just" punishment for convicted defendants, regardless of other consequences or considerations of effectiveness. Some might oppose them because they are triggered by the amount of drugs possessed, not the amount owned or controlled, again without considering other factors.

The opinion of many people might, however, be influenced by an assessment of how well mandatory minimum sentences "work" at controlling drug-related problems. If they could be shown to work well, that might be sufficient to draw support from some who are troubled by the sharp distinction drawn between cocaine powder and crack. If they are shown not to work well, that might give pause to those who value mandatory minimum laws' power to induce plea bargains and cooperation from defendants.

The preceding chapters sought to inform opinions by quantitatively estimating how cost-effective long sentences are for various types of drug dealers at reducing cocaine use, users' spending on cocaine, and cocaine-related crime. To some it may seem strange to evaluate drug sentences in terms of benefits achieved per million taxpayer dollars spent. After all, no legislature votes explicitly on a budget item labeled "extending sentences for dealers who meet the criteria for mandatory minimum sentences." Nevertheless, many public officials make decisions that do lead to more or fewer taxpayer dollars being spent on such sentences. This is most obvious for members of Congress and state legislators. When a new sentencing bill is passed (or repealed), it influences who goes to prison for how long, and incarcerating people costs money. More subtly, prosecutors influence how corrections budgets are divided between mandatory minimum sentences and punishment of other offenders whenever they decide whether to prosecute an arrested dealer or not, or to prosecute the dealer under one statute or another. Heads of enforcement agencies do likewise when they decide how many people to assign to drug control work and whether to target lower-level or higher-level dealing. The more enforcement agents there are, the more drug arrests. The more drug arrests there are, the more long sentences for drug offenders.

The analysis above certainly does not say that drug enforcement should be eliminated, for at least two reasons. First, reducing drug use and related crime and spending are not the only legitimate objectives of drug control. Second, the analysis pertains to relatively modest changes in the scale of drug-control programs. Eliminating federal mandatory minimum drug sentences *would* constitute such a modest change. (Recall that most dealers are convicted in state courts and those convicted in federal courts would still be subject to conventional sentences.) Eliminating all enforcement *would not* be a modest change, and its consequences cannot be inferred by extrapolating the results above.

The analysis above does say, however, that passing and maintaining laws such as the federal mandatory minimum sentencing statutes do not represent an effective or efficient way of reducing drug use, drug spending, or drug-related crime. Conversely, a desire to fight drug use, spending, and crime is not sufficient reason to oppose repealing these laws. It would be perfectly reasonable for someone dedicated to controlling drug use to support repeal of mandatory minimum sentences. That is particularly the case if repeal could be tied to a reallocation of the resources saved into other, more effective drug control programs. Given that one such alternative program is conventional enforcement without mandatory minimum sentences, such a reallocation is not difficult to imagine. It could be achieved, for example, by simultaneously repealing mandatory minimum sentencing laws and expanding the number of enforcement agents, prosecutors, and judges enough to hold constant total spending on drug enforcement.

The title of this report asks whether mandatory minimum drug sentences should be seen as just punishment for heinous offenders ("throwing away the key") or simply as wasteful ("throwing away the taxpayers' money"). Issues of justice cannot be reduced to numbers, so we reviewed the pertinent debate in Chapter Two without drawing conclusions. Issues of efficiency are, however, amenable to quantitative analysis. The preceding chapters show that mandatory minimum drug sentences do throw away taxpayer money in the sense that there are other, more efficient, less costly ways of achieving the same drug control ends.

PART II

Chapter Six

LONGER SENTENCES FOR ALL DRUG DEALERS: DETAILS OF THE DYNAMIC ANALYSIS

This chapter supplements the first section of Chapter Three and is organized the same way. Here, we go into more detail regarding our methodology, repeat the results tables, and offer some more technical detail regarding interpretations. The reader is referred at various points to Chapter Three for full discussion of the results.

The analysis presented here uses the cocaine-control model documented in Rydell and Everingham (1994) to assess the performance of the alternative programs. The analysis is dynamic, recognizing the time pattern of costs and benefits resulting from control program actions. Both supply and demand factors are taken into account. The outputs of the model are the total public cost[1] and the various benefit measures (notably, reduction in cocaine consumption). Treatment of heavy users and conventional enforcement are analyzed here just as they were in that earlier study (except that some parameter estimates—notably the price elasticity of demand—have been revised in light of recent evidence). Analyzing longer sentences, however, required additional information and revisions to the model.

---

[1]By "public cost" we mean cost to the public at large, i.e., to society, as opposed to cost to drug dealers. We do not restrict ourselves to costs to government. Enforcement costs are almost entirely government costs, but some treatment programs are funded by the private sector.

MODELING THE DYNAMICS OF COCAINE CONTROL

As discussed in Chapter Three, the cocaine-control model has two components—one for estimating cocaine demand and the other for analyzing the interaction between demand and supply in the cocaine market. The market component enables comparison of effectiveness of the different control programs on a common outcome measure. We cannot directly compare the proximate accomplishments of supply-controlling enforcement programs (e.g., seizure of cocaine and assets, arrests of dealers) and those of demand-controlling treatment programs (short- or long-term reduction in the number of drug users or the amount of drugs users consume). The accomplishments must first be translated into a common measure of effectiveness. The measure emphasized in this analysis is total consumption of cocaine in the United States. Other measures evaluated include the total number of cocaine users, the total number of heavy cocaine users, and the total user expenditure on cocaine.

Updated Parameter Estimates

Using newly available evidence, we improve upon several of the parameter estimates used in the Rydell and Everingham (1994) analysis. These revised estimates (of course) change the specific estimates of program cost-effectiveness, but (it turns out) do not change the program rankings found in that study.

Price Elasticity of Demand. As mentioned in Chapter Three, enforcement programs, both longer sentences and conventional enforcement, decrease the consumption of cocaine by increasing cocaine's market price. To make the connection between price and consumption one needs estimates of the price elasticity of demand for cocaine, i.e., the percentage change in consumption associated with a 1 percent increase in price. Until recently there were no empirical estimates of this for any illicit drug. Analysts used estimates derived from studies of other dependency-creating substances, namely alcohol and cigarettes. Using the central tendency of the alcohol and cigarette literature reviewed in Manning et al. (1991), Rydell and Everingham (1994) used –0.5, meaning that a 1 percent rise in cocaine price would reduce consumption by 0.5 percent.

Recently, however, four papers have been published that find illicit drugs more responsive to price than the estimate based on licit substances. The first paper is for opium rather than cocaine, and for a non–U.S. population from some time ago (Dutch East Indies, pre–World War II). Van Ours (1995) found the short run elasticity of demand to be –0.7 and the long run elasticity of demand to be –1.0. The other three papers are for cocaine use by the current U.S. population. Using data from DEA's System to Retrieve Information from Drug Evidence (STRIDE) and the National Household Survey on Drug Abuse (NHSDA),[2] Saffer and Chaloupka (1995) estimate elasticities for cocaine of between –0.72 and –1.10. Using data from STRIDE and Monitoring the Future,[3] Grossman, Chaloupka, and Brown (1996) estimate that a permanent 10 percent reduction in cocaine price would lead to a 10 percent increase in the number of cocaine users. They also estimate it would result in a 5 percent increase in frequency of use. Their results thus suggest an overall elasticity of –1.5. Using data from STRIDE and the Drug Use Forecasting System (DUF),[4] Caulkins (1995) estimates that for arrestees, a group responsible for much of the social harm related to drugs, the elasticity for cocaine is between –1.50 and –2.00. In light of this new evidence we now use the estimate that the price elasticity of demand for cocaine is –1.0, meaning that the percentage decrease in consumption equals the percentage increase in price.

Cost of Incarceration. The base-case year for the cocaine-control model is 1992. For that year (and, accordingly, in 1992 dollars) Rydell and Everingham (1994) used the estimate that the average cost in the United States of incarcerating a person for a year was $23,200. However, that estimate was derived from projections of 1992 events. Recently published evidence on actual 1992 events enables us to refine our earlier estimate to a new estimate of $24,972 (see Table 6.1).

---

[2] Sponsored by the National Institute on Drug Abuse (NIDA); measures include number of cocaine users in the U.S. household population.

[3] An annual survey of alcohol, tobacco, and illicit drug use by a representative national sample of 8th, 10th, and 12th graders. The survey is conducted under a NIDA grant to the University of Michigan.

[4] DUF estimates the prevalence of drug use among arrestees in over 20 U.S. cities on a quarterly basis by urinalysis. It is run by the National Institute of Justice.

Table 6.1

Cost of Incarceration in the United States, 1992

Type of Incarceration	U.S. Corrections System, 1992		
	Expenditure ($ million)	Population	Cost Per Prisoner (1992 $)
State and Federal prison	21,162	817,944	25,872
County and Municipal jail	10,299	441,889	23,307
Total	31,461	1,259,833	24,972

SOURCE: Maguire and Pastore (1995), pp. 3 and 6 for expenditures, and pp. 533 and 540 for populations. The jail population is the average daily count during 1992, and the prison population is the average of the December 31, 1991, and the December 31, 1992, counts.

Proportion of Drug Dealers Who Are Also Users. The main effect that incarcerating cocaine dealers has on consumption occurs through price increases. However, some cocaine dealers are also cocaine users, and there is an additional effect on consumption through the incapacitation of dealer-users while they are in prison. Rydell and Everingham (1994) estimated that three-fourths of cocaine dealers are cocaine users, with 0.375 being light cocaine users and 0.375 being heavy cocaine users. We base our estimates for the current analysis on two other sources, one only recently available.

The first of those sources is the DUF. In 1991, 62 percent of those arrested for drug sales tested positive for cocaine, and another 2 percent self-reported either crack or powder cocaine use even though they tested negative. Also, 22.5 percent of males and 30.9 percent of females (25 percent overall) arrested for drug selling reported being dependent on cocaine or crack or reported that they needed treatment for powder cocaine or crack. These data suggest that at least 25 percent of drug sellers are heavy users and another 39 percent are light users. The actual numbers may be higher because (1) not all heavy (i.e., weekly) cocaine users may report being dependent or in need of treatment and (2) some light users (i.e., some who have consumed cocaine within the past year) would not test positive.

However, DUF data pertaining to drug offending arrestees are dominated by low-level drug offenders, so they need to be supplemented with other data. The *Sourcebook* (Maguire and Pastore, 1994, p. 620, Table 6.55) reports that for state prison inmates convicted of drug trafficking, 59.3 percent had used drugs in the month before their offense and 36.2 percent were under the influence of drugs at the time of the offense. These two numbers may be taken to correspond, respectively, to percentages who were users and who were heavy users of some drug—not necessarily cocaine (the difference between the two numbers, 23.1 percent, represents light users).

Based on Table 6.56 in the *Sourcebook* (Maguire and Pastore, 1994, p. 621) one can infer that in 1991 there were 33,765 inmates convicted of drug trafficking who had used cocaine or crack in the month before their offense and 55,631 convicted drug traffickers who had used any drug in the month before their offense. This suggests that about 60 percent of total drug use by drug traffickers is cocaine use. Hence, the *Sourcebook* data suggest that on the order of 22 percent (60 percent × 36.2 percent) of imprisoned drug traffickers are heavy cocaine users and 14 percent (60 percent × 23.1 percent) are light cocaine users.

Averaging the DUF and *Sourcebook* data suggests that half of drug sellers are cocaine users, with 23.5 percent qualifying as heavy users and 26.5 percent as light users.

INCARCERATION OF DRUG DEALERS: REGULAR VERSUS LONGER SENTENCES

To use the cocaine-control model to analyze the cost-effectiveness of longer sentences for drug dealers, we need to estimate both the cost to the public of providing the additional incarceration and the cost imposed on drug dealers by the additional incarceration. Because we discount all costs to present values, estimating incarceration-related costs requires knowing the distribution over time of the additional person-years in prison caused by the longer sentences. Those additional person-years, in turn, depend on the detailed comparison of the longer sentences with the regular sentences in the conventional enforcement program. Accordingly, our analysis of sentencing policy goes through four steps: (a) compare the sentence-length distributions of regular and longer sentences, (b) use the sentence-length distributions to estimate person-years of incarceration by year of sentence, (c) subtract the person-years of incarceration under regular sentences from those under longer sentences to get the additional person-years due to the longer sentences program, and (d) multiply the person-years of incarceration by cost factors (dollars per person-year) to find the distribution over time of public and drug-supplier costs.

The distribution of costs is important because the additional person-years in prison imposed by the longer sentences occur in the future, after the (shorter) regular sentences would have been completed. The significance of this delayed effect becomes apparent when program costs over time are converted into present values as of the start of a program (i.e., the year in which the sentencing occurs). Then, the costs of the extra person-years in prison resulting from longer sentences will receive more discounting than the costs of regular person-years in prison.

Sentence Lengths

Tables 6.2 and 6.3 provide evidence on the sentences received by convicted drug traffickers at the state and federal levels. Table 6.4 averages the state and federal sentencing distributions.[5]

To find the duration of regular sentences (those not greatly influenced by the longer sentences handed out under mandatory minimum policies), we look at the actual sentences served by drug dealers released from prison in 1990.[6] In addition, we need to know the proportion of convicted drug dealers who, under conventional enforcement, do not go to prison because they get probation or only jail sentences.

---

[5]Note that data are from one year, 1990. However, the population is large and, while some variation in terms served might be expected from year to year, we have no reason to believe that 1990 was not representative of the late 1980s and early 1990s. Annual variation in terms served would be unlikely to seriously affect the results presented. (Such a conclusion is demonstrated for the static analysis in Chapters Three and Seven.)

[6]Using data from 1990 is a compromise. Data from earlier years are less relevant because criminal justice procedures and practices vary over time. Data from more recent years contain a larger proportion of people sentenced under mandatory minimums rather than conventional laws.

Table 6.2

Drug Trafficking Convictions by Type of Sentence in the United States, 1990

Type of Sentence	State Courts	Federal Courts	Total
Annual Count			
No incarceration	38,723	2,347	41,070
Jail only	47,141	0	47,141
Prison	82,496	13,841	96,337
Total	168,360	16,188	184,548
Percentage Distribution			
No incarceration	23.0	14.5	22.3
Jail only	28.0	0.0	25.5
Prison	49.0	85.5	52.2
Total	100.0	100.0	100.0

SOURCE: Maguire and Pastore (1994), pp. 510 and 535 for total convictions for drug trafficking during 1990, and pp. 510 and 537 for percentage distribution across type of sentence.

Table 6.3

Distribution of Actual Sentence Lengths That Were Served by Drug Traffickers Released from Prison in the United States, 1990

Sentence served (years)	Percentage Distribution	
	State Prison	Federal Prison
0.5	20.0	15.7
1	30.0	19.0
2	33.7	27.4
3	10.2	20.5
4	3.3	10.0
5	1.3	4.1
6	0.5	1.2
7	0.5	1.2
8	0.5	0.9
9	0.0	0.0
10	0.0	0.0
Total	100.0	100.0

SOURCE: Perkins (1993), p. 27 for state distribution, and p. 70 for federal distribution.

NOTE: The first row is 0.01 to 0.50 years, the second row is 0.51 to 1.00 years, the third row is 1.01 to 2.00 years, and so on.

Table 6.4

Drug Trafficking Convictions by Estimated Actual Sentences Served in the United States, 1990

Length of Sentence (years)	State Courts	Federal Courts	Total
None	38,723	2,347	41,070
0.5	63,640	2,173	65,813
1	24,749	2,630	27,379
2	27,801	3,792	31,594
3	8,415	2,837	11,252
4	2,722	1,384	4,106
5	1,072	567	1,640
6	412	166	579
7	412	166	579
8	412	125	537
9	0	0	0
10	0	0	0
Total	168,360	16,188	184,548

SOURCES: Tables 6.2 and 6.3.

NOTE: The zero count is the no-incarceration count in Table 6.2. The 0.5 count is the jail-only count in Table 6.2 plus the prison count in Table 6.2 times the proportion receiving 0.5-year sentences in Table 6.3. The counts for the rest of the sentence lengths are the prison counts in Table 6.2 distributed as in Table 6.3.

Table 6.2 shows the types of sentences received by drug traffickers in state and federal courts. Note that 91 percent of the convictions are in state courts, so the sentencing pattern there largely determines the total distribution. Those drug dealers who do go to prison under conventional enforcement have the distribution of sentence lengths given in Table 6.3. Note that the evidence here is time actually served by people being released from prison. As such, the reported sentence lengths reflect reductions in nominal sentences due to "good time" regulations, and to early releases caused by prison overcrowding.

Combining the type-of-sentence information in Table 6.2 and the prison-sentence-duration information in Table 6.3 yields the overall sentence distribution in Table 6.4. In constructing this table we assumed that the jail-only sentences in Table 6.2 were for an average of half a year.

Table 6.5 compares this distribution of terms served following regular sentences with those following longer sentences. For the latter, we estimate the result of applying the federal mandatory minimum sentencing law to a representative sample of convicted cocaine dealers.[7] The distribution is based on 1990 and 1991 STRIDE data

Table 6.5

**Estimated Average Sentences Served by Drug Dealers
Convicted in the United States**

Length of Sentence (years)	With Regular Sentences			With Longer Sentences		
	Number of Persons	Persons × Years	Average Sentence (years)	Number of Persons	Persons × Years	Average Sentence (years)
None	41,070	0	0.00	0	0	NA
0.5	65,813	32,907	0.50	0	0	NA
1	27,379	27,379	1.00	0	0	NA
2	31,594	63,187	2.00	0	0	NA
3	11,252	33,756	3.00	0	0	NA
4	4,106	16,426	4.00	0	0	NA
5	1,640	8,200	5.00	122,909	614,545	5.00
6	579	3,471	6.00	0	0	NA
7	579	4,050	7.00	0	0	NA
8	537	4,296	8.00	0	0	NA
9	0	0	NA	0	0	NA
10	0	0	NA	61,639	616,390	10.00
Totals						
All sentences	184,548	193,672	1.05	184,548	1,230,935	6.67
Nonzero sentences	143,478	193,672	1.35	184,548	1,230,935	6.67

NOTES: Distribution of regular sentences is from Table 6.4. Distribution of longer sentences is explained in the text. NA is not applicable.

---

[7]We apply the federal mandatory sentencing scheme here, even though we are interested in dealers arrested in all jurisdictions, because it is necessary to choose one scheme among the many in existence, and the federal allows consistency with the analysis of additional federal enforcement. It could be argued that we should apply a representative state scheme. However, we are more interested in comparing the application of a given scheme to two classes of offenders than in comparing the cost-effectiveness of a representative state policy with that of the federal policy.

on DEA and FBI seizures of powder and crack cocaine: Of the seizures large enough to trigger mandatory minimum sentences, 67.6 percent involved amounts sufficient to trigger 5-year sentences and 32.3 percent, amounts sufficient for 10-year sentences. For this analysis we round these estimates to two-thirds and one-third. Thus, if the 184,548 drug dealers convicted in 1990 in the United States were given longer sentences, the distribution of sentences would be as shown in the third column from the right in Table 6.5.

Multiplying the number of persons sentenced by the number of years in the sentence, summing across all sentence lengths, and then dividing by the total number of persons gives the average sentence length. Under regular sentencing this average is 1.05 years for the average conviction and 1.35 years for the average conviction receiving a nonzero sentence (jail or prison).[8] In contrast, the average longer sentence is 6.67 years, a single number because under the longer-sentences policy all convictions get nonzero sentences.

Cost of Incarceration to the Public and to Drug Suppliers

We take two types of incarceration costs into account. The first is the cost to the public of building and operating the extra prison cells necessary to contain an increase in the average prisoner population. The second is the cost to drug suppliers, by which we mean the amount of money drug suppliers would demand to compensate them for an increased risk of incarceration (either an increased probability of incarceration or an increase in the sentence served if convicted).

To estimate the additional costs caused by the longer sentences, we need to know the public costs in each year beginning with the year in which the million-dollar program is instituted. That expenditure will either put more persons in prison (conventional enforcement) or extend the sentences of those already there (longer sentences). We know costs by person-year of incarceration, so we must first convert

---

[8]These averages for regular sentences differ markedly between state and federal systems. Applying the calculation in Table 6.5 to the state-federal details in Table 6.4 shows that, for all convictions, state sentences average 0.96 years, while federal sentences average 1.94 years, and for convictions with nonzero sentences, state sentences average 1.25 years, while federal sentences average 2.26 years.

the distributions of sentences by sentence length into distributions of person-years of incarceration by year of sentence (i.e., year following program initiation). Then we need to multiply the person-year counts by cost factors (dollars per person-year) representing the cost to the public, and the cost imposed on drug suppliers. Finally, to get costs at the time of the sentencing decision, we need to discount the costs by year of sentence into a present value. Tables 6.6 through 6.8 do this person-year analysis for regular sentences, longer sentences, and the additional sentence lengths caused by the longer sentences. It is, of course, this last variable, the *difference* between longer sentences and regular ones, that will be the basis for calculating the additional costs of longer sentences. We discuss the first column of each of these tables then describe how we arrive at the second and third columns. The NPV (net present value) will also be explained.

Table 6.6 analyzes the person-years of incarceration generated by regular sentences. Person-years accruing in any given sentence year are equal to the persons still incarcerated, i.e., those whose sentences are as long as or longer than that sentence year.[9] For example, on average during the first sentence year of incarceration, the number incarcerated is the sum of two numbers: half of the 65,813 drug dealers with a half-year sentence, and all of the drug dealers with a sentence of one year or more. The first number is then 32,906, and the latter number is the sum of the numbers in the "total" column in Table 6.4 corresponding to sentence lengths of 1 through 8 years, or 77,665. The sum of 32,906 and 77,665 is the 110,571 person-years given for year 1 in Table 6.6. During the second sentence year, the person-years generated are the number of prisoners with sentences of two years or more, or, again, summing from Table 6.4, 50,286. And so on.

Using the distribution of longer sentences (two-thirds 5-year sentences and one-third 10-year sentences), the distribution of person-years for that program is shown in Table 6.7. The total number of persons convicted would now be in prison for 5 years, and one-third of those would be incarcerated for 10. Subtracting the person-years

---

[9]Because not all who serve into a given year serve out the year, the numbers in Table 6.6 have a small upward bias. However, jail time served prior to prison is not counted, and that would result in a small downward bias in the Table 6.6 numbers as a representation of total time incarcerated. The net error in the total person-year counts is probably small.

Table 6.6

Cost of Incarceration to the Public and to Drug Suppliers
for Regular Sentences
(in 1992 dollars)

Year of Sentence	Person-Years of Incarceration	Cost to Public ($ million)	Cost to Suppliers ($ million)
1	110,571	2,761	4,146
2	50,286	1,256	1,886
3	18,693	467	701
4	7,441	186	279
5	3,334	83	125
6	1,694	42	64
7	1,116	28	42
8	537	13	20
9	0	0	0
10	0	0	0
Total	193,672	4,836	7,263
NPV, 4%		4,704	7,063
NPV, 12%			6,733

NOTES: Person-years of incarceration by year of sentence are from sentence-length distribution in Table 6.4. Cost factors for jail and prison costs are from Table 6.1 (cost to the public is $24,972 per person-year) and from the midpoint of the range of estimates in Kleiman (1992), p. 140 (cost to drug suppliers is $37,500 per person-year). NPV at x percent is the sum of these numbers: each year's cost discounted to NPV (year 1) at x percent per year.

from the regular sentences from those from the longer sentences gives the distribution of additional person-years resulting from the longer-sentences program (see Table 6.8).[10]

The effect of longer sentences can best be appreciated graphically. In Figure 6.1, we graph in the light bar segments the number of

---

[10]We assume here that the additional sentence lengths are given to an average mix of regular sentences (i.e., the mix shown in Table 6.4). This may not be the case. For example, if more serious offenders are enforcement priorities, fewer serious offenders meriting shorter sentences are likely to be apprehended if enforcement expands. In that case, the estimated additional person-years of incarceration in Table 6.8 would be an underestimate. However, both the costs and benefits given below for the marginal impact of longer sentences would then be underestimated relative to those of conventional enforcement; so the effect on relative cost-effectiveness is uncertain.

Table 6.7

Cost of Incarceration to the Public and to Drug Suppliers
for Longer Sentences
(in 1992 dollars)

Year of Sentence	Person-Years of Incarceration	Cost to Public ($ million)	Cost to Suppliers ($ million)
1	184,548	4,609	6,921
2	184,548	4,609	6,921
3	184,548	4,609	6,921
4	184,548	4,609	6,921
5	184,548	4,609	6,921
6	61,454	1,535	2,305
7	61,454	1,535	2,305
8	61,454	1,535	2,305
9	61,454	1,535	2,305
10	61,454	1,535	2,305
Total	1,230,012	30,716	46,125
NPV, 4%		27,177	40,811
NPV, 12%			33,220

NOTES: Person-years of incarceration by year of sentence are from the sentence-length distribution in Table 6.5. Cost factors for jail and prison costs are
from Table 6.1 (cost to the public is $24,972 per person-year) and from the
midpoint of the range of estimates in Kleiman (1992), p. 140 (cost to drug
suppliers is $37,500 per person-year). For NPV, see Table 6.6.

person-years generated in each year following a year's imposition of
regular sentences (segment heights equal to the "person-years of incarceration" numbers in Table 6.6). As in preceding tables, the
number and distribution of imposed sentences match those of the
terms actually completed across the nation in 1990. The dark portion
of the bars in Figure 6.1 shows the distribution of the additional
person-years incarceration if the actual 1990 exit distribution is replaced by a two-to-one mix of 5- and 10-year terms (from "person-
years of incarceration" numbers in Table 6.8; the full heights of the
bars are, of course, equal to the analogous numbers in Table 6.7).
Comparing the additional person-years with those from regular
sentences shows that relatively few of the additional person-years
occur in the early years of the sentence. The distribution of person-
years for the average sentences peaks in the first year, while the peak
of the distribution for the additional person-years due to longer sentences does not occur until the fifth year. This lag means that the

Table 6.8

**Cost of Incarceration to the Public and to Drug Suppliers
for the Additional Length of Longer Sentences
(in 1992 dollars)**

Year of Sentence	Person-Years of Incarceration	Cost to Public ($ million)	Cost to Suppliers ($ million)
1	73,977	1,847	2,774
2	134,262	3,353	5,035
3	165,855	4,142	6,220
4	177,107	4,423	6,642
5	181,214	4,525	6,796
6	59,760	1,492	2,241
7	60,339	1,507	2,263
8	60,917	1,521	2,284
9	61,454	1,535	2,305
10	61,454	1,535	2,305
Total	1,036,341	25,880	38,863
NPV, 4%		22,474	33,748
NPV, 12%			26,487

NOTES: Person-years of incarceration by year of sentence are from the difference of the distributions in Tables 6.6 and 6.7. Cost factors for jail and prison costs are from Table 6.1 (cost to the public is $24,972 per person-year) and from the midpoint of the range of estimates in Kleiman (1992), p. 140 (cost to drug suppliers is $37,500 per person-year).

added costs of the longer-sentences program tend to occur later than the costs of conventional enforcement, and that fact is important in evaluating the program's cost-effectiveness.

To arrive at the numbers in the second and third columns of Tables 6.6 through 6.8, we apply cost factors to the person-year counts. For public cost, we use a figure of $24,972 per person-year of incarceration, as discussed above. We wish to equate dealer cost to the additional revenue dealers demand to compensate them for their increased risk of incarceration under increased enforcement. No one knows how much dealers demand as compensation for the risk of spending a year in prison, but there are at least two guesses in the literature. One of those is for high-level dealers, and we will use that in the next chapter. For the typical dealers we are concerned with here, we use $37,500 per person-year of incarceration. The latter is

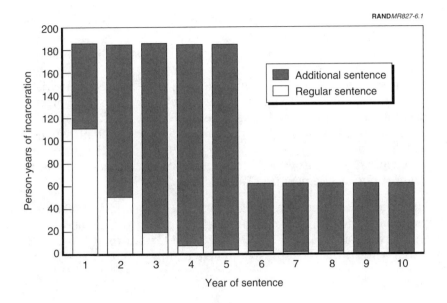

**Figure 6.1—Person-Years of Incarceration from Regular
and Longer Sentences**

the middle of the range given by Kleiman (1992, p. 140),[11] who
asserts,

> What a potential cocaine dealer needs to be paid to incur a prison
> risk equivalent to the certainty of a year in prison is anyone's guess;
> it is likely to vary widely depending on the dealer's alternative out-
> side the industry, but $25,000 to $50,000 per year seems to be a
> reasonable range (roughly equal to 1 percent chance of sudden
> death).

Cost factor application yields the columns with the estimated public
and supplier costs of incarceration by year of sentence. Each of these
cost streams can be collapsed to one number by discounting each
year's cost to find its NPV and adding up the NPVs. For the cost to

---

[11]Kleiman's numbers apply to all offenders. That we do not have such an estimate for
those meeting mandatory minimum triggering amounts is one of the principal
barriers to a state- and local-level mandatory minimum analysis.

the public, we assume a real social discount rate (i.e., over and above any inflation adjustment) of 4 percent.[12]   For drug dealers, we assume a real discount rate of 12 percent. We speculate that drug dealers may, to a greater extent than society as a whole, prefer their rewards in the near term, because they objectively face greater risks and, hence, should downplay future outcomes. More important, they tend to be young (and youth also seem more interested in near-term rewards) and have by their actions eschewed legitimate careers, which are more likely to involve delayed gratification. For purposes of sensitivity analysis, we also compute costs to drug suppliers using a dealer rate of 4 percent (see Table 6.9).

Under a dealer discount rate of 12 percent, a one million dollar program paying for longer sentences causes supplier costs to increase by $1.179 million ($1M × $26,487M/$22,474M, from the third row of Table 6.9). If the dealer discount rate is only 4 percent, then a $1

Table 6.9

**Discounted Costs of Incarceration to the Public and
to Drug Suppliers in the United States
(in 1992 dollars)**

Type of Sentence	Person-Years of Incarceration	Cost to Public (discount rate 4%)	Cost to Suppliers (discount rate 4%)	(discount rate 12%)
		Total Cost ($ million)		
Regular	193,672	4,704	7,063	6,733
Longer (total)	1,230,012	27,177	40,811	33,220
Longer (additional)	1,036,341	22,474	33,748	26,487
		Cost Per Person-Year ($)		
Regular	193,672	24,287	36,470	34,767
Longer (total)	1,230,012	22,095	33,180	27,008
Longer (additional)	1,036,341	21,686	32,565	25,558

SOURCES: Tables 6.6, 6.7, and 6.8.

---

[12]Choice of discount rate is the subject of a considerable literature. The 4 percent used here falls within the range of those commonly used in public policy analysis and allows comparability with previous analyses in which we have used that rate.

million program paying for longer sentences causes supplier costs of $1.502 million. Our analysis focuses on discounted costs of the additional sentence lengths because it assumes that the cost to suppliers over all sentence years affects suppliers immediately when the sentence is imposed. The cost that is passed through to consumers as a cocaine price increase is the compensation suppliers must pay to make drug dealers bear the added risk of incarceration. That risk can be expressed in terms of the discounted value of the additional prison time dealers will receive. They will want an immediate risk premium equivalent to the cost to them of their entire expected sentence.

REDUCTION OF COCAINE CONSUMPTION BY ALTERNATIVE PROGRAMS

Having found the cost to the public of providing additional incarceration, and the cost such provision imposes on drug suppliers, we now turn to what effect this has on cocaine consumption. The Rydell and Everingham (1994) cocaine-control model enables us to trace how the market effects of the added costs to suppliers cause the price of cocaine to increase, and the consumption of cocaine to decrease.[13] That model also enables us to assess the performance of the treatment and conventional-enforcement programs.

For each program, we estimate a 15-year stream of benefits and costs discounted to present value. Fifteen years is typical of the periods used in the analysis of public policies. However, some may be interested in a nearer future, so we also present nearer-term costs and

---

[13]In the runs of the cocaine-control model for this current analysis, several parameter estimates have been updated from those given in Appendix E of Rydell and Everingham (1994), as discussed in the first part of this section. Price elasticity of demand: in Figure E.4 "e" changed from –0.5 to –1.0. Cost of incarceration to public and to suppliers: in Figure E.5 DoPrisonCostRate changed from 0.0232 to 0.0243, and DoPrisonSanctRate changed from 0.0386 to 0.0348. (Note the model's specification of cost factors in millions of dollars is discounted to the initial program year, so the $0.0243 million public cost per person-year of incarceration in initial-year dollars is equivalent to $0.024972 million per person-year at the time of the incarceration, and the $0.0348 million supplier cost per person-year of incarceration is equivalent to $0.0375 million per person-year at the time of the incarceration.) Proportion dealers who are light and heavy cocaine users: in Figure E.6 PropLiDealers changed from 0.375 to 0.265 and PropHeDealers changed from 0.375 to 0.235.

benefits. For purposes of comparison across alternative programs, we report the effect on consumption per million dollars spent on each program.

Program Costs

Table 6.10 shows how the public costs of the alternative programs vary by cohort year.[14] The costs are normalized to represent programs with a discounted cost of one million dollars over a 15-year

Table 6.10

Costs to the Public by Cohort Year of Alternative Million-Dollar Programs

Cohort Year	Public Cost ($ million)		
	Treatment of Heavy Users	Conventional Enforcement	Longer Sentences
1	1.000	0.860	0.082
2	0.000	0.091	0.149
3	0.000	0.034	0.184
4	0.000	0.013	0.197
5	0.000	0.006	0.201
6	0.000	0.003	0.066
7	0.000	0.002	0.067
8	0.000	0.001	0.068
9	0.000	0.000	0.068
10	0.000	0.000	0.068
11	0.000	0.000	0.000
12	0.000	0.000	0.000
13	0.000	0.000	0.000
14	0.000	0.000	0.000
15	0.000	0.000	0.000
NPV, 4%	1.000	1.000	1.000

SOURCES: Tables 6.6 and 6.8.

NOTE: For rationale behind distribution of cost streams, see text.

---

[14]"Cohort year" is the year after treatment for the treatment program (with treatment occurring in the first year), and the year after sentencing for the enforcement programs (with incarceration starting in the first year).

evaluation period.[15] The public costs of treatment all occur in the first cohort year. The public costs for conventional enforcement result from seizure and arrest costs, which occur in the first cohort year, and incarceration costs, which are distributed as the costs of the regular sentences in Table 6.6. That is, we first put two-thirds of the enforcement cost in year one.[16] Then we distribute, in proportion to the yearly entries in the "cost to public" column in Table 6.6, an amount for incarceration that will yield an NPV of a third of a million dollars. The distribution of (additional) public costs from the longer sentences program is from Table 6.8, with the amount distributed sufficient to generate an NPV of $1 million.

Note the progression from treatment costs occurring entirely in the first year, to conventional enforcement costs concentrated in the first few cohort years, to the additional costs of longer sentences not peaking until the fifth year. This contrast in cost profiles is important in understanding how the length of the evaluation period affects cost-effectiveness estimates (see below).

Program Benefits

Table 6.11 gives the model's principal output—the decrease in cocaine consumption per million dollars spent on each of the three control programs. These results are fully discussed in Chapter Three.

We note here that treatment is about four times more cost-effective at the margin than conventional enforcement. This is lower than the seven times more cost-effective reported in our previous analysis of these two programs (Rydell and Everingham, 1994, Table 3.2, p. 24) because we have since increased our estimate of how responsive cocaine demand is to changes in price. Specifically, we formerly assumed that a 1 percent price increase caused a 1/2 percent decrease

---

[15]To give some sense of the relative size of a million-dollar program, Rydell and Everingham (1994, Table B.8, p. 70) estimate annual public expenditure on "domestic enforcement" for cocaine in the United States to be approximately $9.5 billion.

[16]Rydell and Everingham (1994, Table B.8, p. 70) break total cocaine enforcement expenditure down to $6.25 billion for agency costs, net of revenue from forfeited assets, but including court costs, and $3.22 billion for corrections costs, for a ratio of roughly 2 to 1.

Table 6.11

Cocaine Consumption Averted by Cohort Year of Alternative Million-Dollar Programs

Cohort Year	Kilograms of Consumption Averted Per Million Dollars Spent on Each Program		
	Treatment of Heavy Users	Conventional Enforcement	Longer Sentences
1	17.496	12.493	5.636
2	8.561	1.379	0.645
3	8.486	1.400	0.655
4	8.414	1.415	0.662
5	8.346	1.426	0.667
6	8.278	1.434	0.671
7	8.212	1.438	0.673
8	8.145	1.439	0.673
9	8.078	1.438	0.673
10	8.009	1.435	0.671
11	7.939	1.429	0.669
12	7.866	1.422	0.666
13	7.792	1.414	0.662
14	7.716	1.404	0.657
15	7.637	1.393	0.652
NPV, 4%	103.584	27.479	12.648

SOURCE: Runs of the revised cocaine-control model, with a 15-year evaluation horizon, a $37,500 per person-year cost of incarceration to suppliers, a 12 percent dealer discount rate, and a –1.0 price elasticity of demand.

in consumption, and now we assume that a 1 percent price increase causes a 1 percent decrease in consumption.[17] This change increases the estimated effectiveness of supply-control programs from that found by the earlier analysis.

Sources of Costs and Benefits

Models are valuable because they take into account many interrelated processes simultaneously, but, for that reason, the causes of

---

[17]See the above discussion of updated parameter estimates for the cocaine-control model. The other parameter updates also contribute to the revised results, but the effects of those revisions are relatively small.

their output are often difficult to discern. To increase our understanding of the sources of each program's costs and benefits, we perform here an approximate summary analysis. We can also learn something from the difference between the results of this analysis and that performed by the model.

Longer sentences impose costs on dealers only through incarceration and do so at a rate of $1.50 per program dollar spent (because the cost imposed on dealers is $37,500 per person-year of incarceration and the cost to the government is about $25,000). Thus, longer sentences drive cocaine costs up by $1.5 million per million taxpayer dollars spent. Divided by the $37.6 billion annual gross revenue from retail cocaine sales in the United States,[18] this translates into a 0.004 percent increase in the price of cocaine. We assume, as noted above, that a 1 percent increase in the price of cocaine results in a 1 percent decrease in consumption. Thus, we multiply 0.004 percent by the 291,000 kilos of cocaine consumed annually in the United States. We obtain an estimate that one million dollars spent on the longer-sentences program causes an 11.6-kilogram reduction in consumption. The cocaine-control model takes account of the interaction between this new program added at the margin and the levels of existing control programs. In essence, by shrinking the market, the preexisting enforcement pressure is spread over a smaller target and so becomes more effective than it was previously without the new program. The model also counts the reduction in use from incarcerating dealers who are also users. Finally, the model discounts, which works to *reduce* the cost-effectiveness, since the benefit is subject to the dealer discount rate, which is higher than the social rate by which the cost is discounted. On net, we find with the model that the new program's effect per million program dollars is actually a little larger than that just estimated, namely the 12.6-kilogram reduction reported in Table 6.11.

In contrast, one million dollars spent on conventional cocaine enforcement causes a 27.5-kilogram reduction in cocaine consumption. This comes about in two stages. First, two-thirds of the one million dollars pays police and other government agencies to arrest

---

[18]According to Rydell and Everingham (1994), 291,000 kilos per year at $129.20 per gram. See Appendix B for a discussion of the size of the U.S. cocaine market.

drug dealers, seizing their cocaine and some of their assets. This first two-thirds of a million imposes a $2.25 million cost on suppliers (because $3.41 million cost is imposed per million public program dollars spent on this stage[19]). Second, the remaining one-third of the overall million dollars of public expenditure goes to pay for 1.35-year sentences for those arrested drug dealers who are convicted and sent to jail or prison (see Table 6.5). This last one-third of a million imposes a half-million-dollar cost on suppliers (because $1.5 million is imposed per million public program dollars spent on this stage). So, a million dollars of public expenditure spent on the seizure and imprisonment stages together results in a total cost to suppliers of $2.75 million (2.25 + 0.5). Dividing by $37.6 billion gross revenue from cocaine sales, to get a 0.0073 percent price increase, and applying that percentage to the 291,000-kilogram annual cocaine consumption, yields an estimated 21.3-kilogram reduction in cocaine consumption. Using the cocaine-control model to take account of the interaction between this increment to supply control at the margin and the levels of existing control programs, we find that the effect is about 30 percent larger than our approximate calculation, namely the 27.5-kilogram reduction reported in Table 6.11.

Finally, we need to look at why treatment performs so well. Only an estimated 13 percent of heavy cocaine users stop heavy use after completing the average treatment program (see Table 6.12). So, how can treatment be so cost-effective? The answer lies partly in the fact that a large percentage of those treated (an estimated 79 percent) are off cocaine while they are in the treatment program (which lasts an average of 0.30 years), but mostly in the fact that the average treatment does not cost very much (only $1,740 for the average mix of residential and outpatient treatments).[20]

---

[19]The $3.41 million is derived as follows. Rydell and Everingham (1994, Table B.6, p. 68 and Table B.10, p. 71) show that domestic cocaine enforcement annually imposes an estimated cost on dealers of $21.3 billion in product seizures, asset seizures, and arrest sanctions (i.e., time and attorney costs incident to arrest). These seizure and arrest sanctions come at a cost to the public of $6.25 billion, and 21.3/6.25 = 3.41.

[20]Part of the reason the cost is so low is that many treatments end early when a client quits the program, often after just a few days or weeks (of course, such failures also contribute to the low long-term success rate).

Table 6.12

Treatment Program Characteristics

Characteristic	Type of Treatment		
	Outpatient	Residential	All
Percentage of all treatments (1992)	77.5	22.5	100.0
Percentage of all heavy users (1992)	24.5	7.1	31.6
Cost per treatment (1992 dollars)	762	5,107	1,740
Treatment duration (years)	0.280	0.410	0.309
Cost per person-year (1992 dollars)	2,722	12,467	5,626
Percentage off drugs during treatment	73	99	79
Percentage exiting heavy use	12.2	16.7	13.2

SOURCE: Rydell and Everingham (1994).

At $1,740 per treatment, one million dollars is enough to treat 575 heavy cocaine users. This number treated, times 79 percent abstinence during treatment for an average of 0.30 years, times 0.12 kilograms per year consumed by the average heavy user (Everingham and Rydell, 1994, p. 48) amounts to a 16-kilogram reduction in U.S. consumption in the first year. We then multiply the 575 heavy users treated by 13 percent (the percentage who stop using cocaine over the long term), by 14 years (the remainder of the evaluation period), and again by 0.12 kilograms per year. The result is an additional reduction of 126 kilograms in consumption over the remaining 14 years of the evaluation period. So, the total estimated reduction from the one million dollars public expenditure on treatment is 142 kilograms (16 from during the program and 126 from after the program).

The 142-kilogram reduction estimated by this approximate calculation is higher than the 103.6-kilogram reduction estimated using the cocaine-control model and reported in Table 6.11. There are three reasons why the approximate calculation is higher. First, some cocaine abusers stop heavy use without treatment (see Figure 3.1, exits to light use and no use). The model counts only exits from heavy use above this background level as program accomplishments. Second, not all users who stop heavy use after treatment do so permanently. Some merely retreat temporarily to light use and then later return to heavy use. Again, the model accounts for this return (see Figure 3.1).

Third, and finally, the model discounts (at an annual real social discount rate of 4 percent) the consumption reductions that stretch out into the future to correctly compare them with the treatment cost that is incurred in the first year of a treatment cohort.

EFFECT OF EVALUATION HORIZON AND SUPPLIER COST OF INCARCERATION

The finding that the longer-sentences program is less cost-effective than alternative programs depends upon the evaluation horizon used in the analysis, and on the decision to evaluate the program's performance when targeted on the average convicted cocaine dealer. Decreasing the evaluation horizon, or targeting the program on higher-level dealers (who require higher-risk premiums), would increase the relative cost-effectiveness of the longer-sentences program. However, as the following threshold analyses show, one has to move a considerable distance in these directions to change the program rankings reported in Table 6.11.

The above cost-effectiveness results assume that programs are evaluated over a 15-year period. Political considerations sometimes encourage shorter evaluation horizons. To show the effect that truncating the evaluation horizon can have, Table 6.13 varies that horizon from 1 to 15 years.

Our analysis assumes the average dealer risk premium to be $37,500 per year (in 1992 dollars). Table 6.14 shows the effect of varying the supplier cost of incarceration for the additional person-years of incarceration caused by the longer-sentences program from $0 to $350,000. (The two excursions in this section are graphed and more fully discussed in Chapter Three.)

SENSITIVITY TO UNCERTAIN PARAMETERS

In the above threshold analysis, the supplier cost of incarceration is a program-design parameter—targeting the longer-sentences program on higher-level drug dealers increases the costs imposed on suppliers for that program. However, we also need to view the supplier cost as an uncertain parameter. The source of our $37,500 per person-year estimate is Kleiman (1992), who considers plausible a

Table 6.13

Program Cost-Effectiveness by Evaluation Horizon

Evaluation Horizon (years)	Kilograms of Consumption Averted Per Million Dollars Spent on Each Program		
	Treatment of Heavy Users	Conventional Enforcement	Longer Sentences
1	17.5	14.5	68.6
2	25.7	14.6	27.7
3	33.6	15.5	17.3
4	41.1	16.5	13.0
5	48.2	17.7	10.8
6	55.0	18.8	10.7
7	61.5	19.9	10.7
8	67.7	21.0	10.7
9	73.6	22.0	10.6
10	79.2	23.1	10.6
11	84.6	24.0	11.0
12	89.7	24.9	11.5
13	94.5	25.8	11.9
14	99.2	26.7	12.3
15	103.6	27.5	12.6

SOURCES: Tables 6.10 and 6.11.

NOTE: Discounted value of the cumulative consumption number from Table 6.11 is divided by discounted value of the cumulative cost number from Table 6.10, through the same evaluation year.

range of $25,000 to $50,000. In testing the effect that varying this parameter has on our conclusions, we need to vary it in the analysis of conventional enforcement as well as in the analysis of longer sentences. Moreover, since this parameter affects reference-situation market behavior, our estimate of the cost-effectiveness of treatment will change slightly also.

Table 6.15 reports the results of this and other sensitivity analyses. Note that the price elasticity of demand affects both treatment and enforcement because it affects the way supply and demand interact in the market. Note also that varying the supplier cost of incarceration (either as such or through the dealer discount rate) affects the performance of the longer-sentences program more than that of

Table 6.14

Program Cost-Effectiveness by Supplier Cost of Additional Incarceration from Longer Sentences

Supplier Cost of Longer Sentences ($ per person-year)	Kilograms of Consumption Averted Per Million Dollars Spent on Each Program		
	Treatment of Heavy Users	Conventional Enforcement	Longer Sentences
0	103.6	27.5	0.0
25,000	103.6	27.5	8.4
50,000	103.6	27.5	16.9
75,000	103.6	27.5	25.3
100,000	103.6	27.5	33.7
125,000	103.6	27.5	42.2
150,000	103.6	27.5	50.6
175,000	103.6	27.5	59.0
200,000	103.6	27.5	67.5
225,000	103.6	27.5	75.9
250,000	103.6	27.5	84.3
275,000	103.6	27.5	92.8
300,000	103.6	27.5	101.2
325,000	103.6	27.5	109.6
350,000	103.6	27.5	118.0

SOURCE: Treatment and conventional enforcement results are the same as in the last row of Table 6.13. Longer sentence results are from runs of the revised cocaine-control model.

conventional enforcement. This is because incarceration is the sole way that lengthening sentences affects supplier costs, while it is only one among several ways that conventional enforcement affects supplier costs. For further discussion, see Chapter Three.

ALTERNATIVE EVALUATION CRITERIA

We find that the program rankings are similar for various benefit measures (see Table 6.16). Per million dollars, longer sentences reduce consumption, user-years, and heavy-user-years less than conventional enforcement does, and both enforcement approaches reduce them less than treatment does. On the user expenditure criterion, however, conventional enforcement is, marginally, the least successful. Treatment decreases user expenditures, while the enforcement programs have essentially no effect.

Table 6.15

Effect of Alternative Parameter Estimates on Consumption Results

	Parameter Estimates			Kilograms of Consumption Averted Per Million Dollars Spent on Each Program		
Assumptions	Price Elasticity of Demand	Supplier Cost of Incapacitation ($ per person-year)	Dealer Discount Rate (%)	Treatment of Heavy Users	Conventional Enforcement	Longer Sentences
Base-Case Analysis						
Base-case estimates	−1.0	37,500	12	103.6	27.5	12.6
Sensitivity to price elasticity of demand for cocaine						
Low elasticity	**−0.5**	37,500	12	88.0	11.7	5.3
High elasticity	**−1.5**	37,500	12	124.7	50.3	23.2
Sensitivity to supplier cost of incarceration						
Low supplier cost	−1.0	**25,000**	12	102.7	26.9	8.7
High supplier cost	−1.0	**50,000**	12	104.3	28.0	16.4
Sensitivity to annual dealer discount rate						
High dealer discount	−1.0	37,500	**20**	103.5	27.4	10.4
Low dealer discount	−1.0	37,500	**4**	103.7	27.6	16.0
Sensitivity to extreme combinations of parameters						
Favoring alternative programs	**−0.5**	**25,000**	**20**	87.7	11.5	3.0
Favoring longer sentences	**−1.5**	**50,000**	**4**	127.3	51.9	38.8

SOURCE: Runs of the revised cocaine-control model.
NOTE: Bold indicates parameter changes from base case.

Table 6.16

Comparing Programs According to Alternative Evaluation Criteria

Outcome	Changes in Outcome Per Million Dollars Spent on Each Program		
	Treatment of Heavy Users	Conventional Enforcement	Longer Sentences
Cocaine consumption (kilograms)	−103.6	−27.5	−12.6
User expenditure on cocaine ($ million)	−8.64	0.20	0.12
Number of cocaine user-years	−586	−253	−118
Number of heavy-cocaine-user-years	−587	−81	−38

SOURCE: Runs of the revised cocaine-control model.

Note that heavy users account for the entire effect of treatment on all users,[21] but only a fraction of enforcement's effect on all users. This happens because treatment is focused on heavy users, while enforcement's effect (via increases in the price of cocaine) influences the behavior of both light and heavy users.

---

[21]In fact, treatment decreases heavy users slightly more than it decreases total users because some treated heavy users reduce but do not cease cocaine use, so they become light users.

Chapter Seven

MANDATORY MINIMUMS FOR FEDERALLY PROSECUTED DRUG DEALERS: DETAILS OF THE STATIC ANALYSIS

This chapter supplements the second section of Chapter Three and is organized the same way. Here, we go into more detail regarding our methodology, repeat the results tables, and offer some more-technical detail regarding interpretations and further sensitivity analysis. The reader is referred at various points to Chapter Three for full discussion of the results.

Recall, once more, our three alternatives: mandatory minimums, conventional enforcement, and treatment of heavy users, with the first two targeted at federal-level offenders possessing enough cocaine to trigger a federal mandatory minimum sentence. The last of these is analyzed as it was in Chapter Six. A convenient way to think about expanding the imposition of traditional sentences is to imagine imposing them on more people, by arresting, trying, convicting, and sentencing more offenders. For the alternative, imagine prosecuting, convicting, and sentencing already-arrested offenders under mandatory minimum sentences instead of traditional sentences. Note that we define the costs and effects of mandatory minimums as the difference between the costs and effects under the two sentencing regimes. For that reason and for convenience of calculation, we will estimate the costs and effects of mandatory minimums by, first, estimating those of arresting, trying, convicting, and sentencing more offenders, although to longer sentences. We can then "subtract" the results for conventional sentences from these estimates of mandatory minimum sentences to obtain the cost and consequences of simply imposing mandatory minimum sentences on people who would be arrested anyway without further expansion of police-level enforcement resources.

This approach is depicted graphically in Figure 7.1. Panel A shows, in the large, unhatched box, that, under a hypothetical baseline prospective enforcement budget without mandatory minimums, some number of people n will be arrested and receive the average sentence shown. (The average sentence takes into account that some of those arrested will not serve time.) The hatched box depicts the effect of adding $1 million to that budget. The effect is the arrest of Δn_1 persons for the prevailing average sentence. It is our purpose in this chapter to evaluate that Δn_1—and to estimate additional effects such as seizure of arrestees' assets.

In panel B of Figure 7.1, we superimpose on panel A the effect of devoting the additional $1 million to arrest, prosecution, and incarceration under mandatory minimum sentences. This would result in longer sentences and, since much of the extra million dollars would be needed to fund those longer terms, fewer additional persons (Δn_2) could be arrested.

However, we are really interested in the relative cost-effectiveness of mandatory minimum *sentences*. We do not want to charge the costs or credit the benefits of extending the baseline conventional-enforcement regime to the account of mandatory minimums. Thus, what we are really interested in is the hatched box in panel C: How many more persons can we incarcerate if another million dollars were spent on extending to mandatory minimum lengths the sentences of those who will be arrested anyway under the baseline budget? That number of persons will be larger than Δn_2, because money spent on arrest in panel B could now be spent on incarceration. It can be calculated as $1 million divided by the difference in per-person costs in panels B and A.

The graphs shown in Figure 7.1 could also represent the relations among the alternative approaches with respect to costs or to consequences other than sentence length. In all cases, the costs or consequences resulting from a single arrest would be represented by the height of the hatched box. For additional conventional enforcement, that would be the height of the box in panel A. For mandatory minimums, it would be the height of the box in panel C, or, as we will calculate it, the height of the box in panel B minus that of the box in panel A. Total costs or consequences would be determined by multiplying the per-arrest costs or consequences by the number of ar-

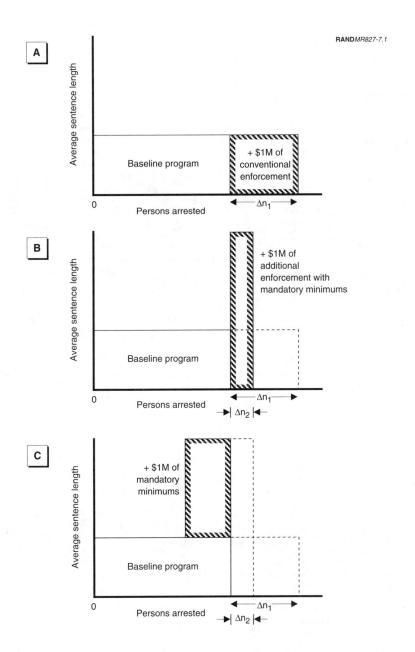

RAND*MR827-7.1*

Figure 7.1—Representation of Conventional Enforcement and Mandatory
Minimum Alternatives

rests indicated by the width of the hatched box in panel A (conventional enforcement) or panel C (mandatory minimums).

MODELING STRATEGY

In the following subsections, we first review our two-stage modeling approach in general terms and then discuss each stage in detail.

First Stage: Consequences and Public Cost of Interventions

In modeling federal-level enforcement with conventional or mandatory minimum sentences, the unit of analysis is an arrest of someone in possession of enough cocaine to trigger a mandatory minimum sentence. We refer to such an arrest as a "qualifying arrest" to distinguish it from a typical drug arrest. We estimate, for a qualifying arrest

- all of the associated dollar costs to the government incurred by enforcement agencies, courts, and corrections

- all of the consequences in terms of cocaine seized, assets seized, years served in prison by offenders, and so on.

Dividing the vector of consequences by the cost yields the outcomes per dollar spent. As in Chapter Six, we multiply by one million, which yields outcomes per million dollars spent.

For example, suppose that a typical qualifying arrest followed by regular sentencing costs the federal government $40,000 and generates a vector of consequences X_1. Then spending a million dollars arresting people who qualify for mandatory minimum sentences but instead imposing regular sentences on them would generate consequences of $25X_1$. Suppose further that a typical qualifying arrest followed by sentencing under the mandatory minimum rules costs $100,000 and generates a vector of consequences X_2. Then spending a million dollars arresting people and imposing mandatory minimum sentences would generate consequences of $10X_2$. Note: in this case it costs $60,000 more to impose mandatory minimum sentences than it does to impose conventional sentences. Call the consequences of doing so X_3 (where $X_3 = X_2 - X_1$). Then a million dollars would be enough to shift the prosecution of 16.7 already arrested drug dealers from a conventional-sentencing regime to a mandatory minimum sentencing regime.

We would say that arresting drug dealers and imposing conventional sentencing is more cost-effective than arresting them and imposing mandatory minimum sentences if $25X_1$ is "greater" than $10X_2$. Likewise, we would say that conventional enforcement is more cost-effective than imposing mandatory minimum sentences if $25X_1$ is greater than $16.7X_3$.

Of course we cannot make such a comparison directly because $25X_1$, $10X_2$ and $16.7X_3$ are vectors, or collections of outcomes, not single numbers. To facilitate direct comparison, we denominate all outcomes (except for quantities of cocaine demanded) in dollars. For example, an increase in the time a dealer spends incarcerated is expressed in terms of how much income a dealer would be willing to give up to avoid that increase.

For treatment, we simply reproduce the base-case effectiveness found in Chapter Six. Thus the base-case results for treatment in this chapter present no new information. However, including treatment in this static model allows us to examine how the relative efficacy of all three interventions depends on various parameters.

Second Stage: Effects on the Market

The second stage of the model takes as inputs the number of heavy-user-years of demand averted[1] and the vectors of consequences of arrest and incarceration and estimates their impact on the quantity of cocaine sold and the price at which it is sold. Note that the use of

---

[1] In this chapter, a "heavy-user-year" is a measure of annual cocaine demand equivalent to that generated by a heavy user. Thus, a heavy user creates a demand of one heavy-user-year of cocaine per year he or she is free on the street, while a light user generates demand equivalent to an eighth of a heavy-user-year annually (Everingham and Rydell, 1994). We use heavy-user-years instead of grams to describe intermediate consequences of additional program expenditures. The reason for this is that a program's immediate effect is on demand (i.e., the demand curve), not consumption; the effect on consumption is found in the second stage by interacting demand with supply. (If the price is near the reference point, demand and consumption are equal, so we refer in the text to heavy-user-years of consumption.) Note this usage differs from that in Table 3.3 (6.16), where "heavy-user-years" refers to consumption by heavy users only.

these two summary measures—quantity and price—implicitly assumes that the interventions in question do not affect the nondollar costs of using drugs, most notably the "search time" or amount of effort required to obtain the drug. This assumption is justified for at least two reasons. First, although interventions have affected the price and purity of cocaine (e.g., in late 1989 and early 1990), we do not have any evidence that they have ever made cocaine physically hard to find. Second, it is local enforcement targeted at retail markets that has been suggested as having potential to raise search time costs. However, mandatory minimum sentences rarely apply to retail dealers, because the amounts they have in their possession are generally less than the quantities (500 grams of powder or 5 grams of crack at the federal level) required to trigger those sentences.

The present model, like any market model, has a demand curve and a supply curve. The demand curve is assumed to be linear through the current equilibrium and is characterized by its elasticity of demand, or the responsiveness of consumption to changes in price, at the current equilibrium. Of course the entire demand curve is almost certainly not linear, but we need to model only the small segment of the demand curve very close to the current level of consumption, and a straight line approximation is reasonable for that small segment. We care about only that small segment because we are trying to estimate the cost-effectiveness of spending an additional million dollars, which can be regarded as marginal relative to the billions of dollars spent on cocaine control annually.

Modeling the supply curve requires less innocuous assumptions. Recall that the supply curve gives the prices per unit required to call forth from suppliers a given quantity of cocaine. The basic premise of this analysis is that made by Reuter and Kleiman (1986) in their "risks and prices" analysis, namely, that those prices just compensate suppliers for all of the costs they incur, including both monetary and nonmonetary costs. That is, we assume that because of low barriers to entry and low technological requirements, free entry will ensure that, in the long run, drug suppliers do not make any supernormal profits. This reduces the quantity-price relation to a quantity-cost relation.

(Obviously accounting profits, i.e., dollar profits, in the drug industry are substantial; this assumption in no way denies that. It merely states that those accounting profits are compensation for the non-monetary costs of participating in the drug trade, such as the risk of arrest and incarceration, the risk of injury or death at the hands of other market participants, the value of one's own time, lost future earning potential in the licit market, normal return on investment, etc. Reuter, MacCoun, and Murphy (1990), studying dollar flows and risks incurred for retail cocaine dealers in Washington, D.C. suggest that economic profits, which are net of monetary *and nonmonetary* costs, are indeed much smaller than accounting profits.[2])

To obtain the supply curve, we thus need to know costs. We divide costs into three categories—costs proportional to the quantity of drugs sold, to the value of drugs sold, and to enforcement spending—and we estimate the relative magnitudes of these costs. It is then a simple exercise in calculus to compute how cocaine consumption, price, and spending will respond to spending a million dollars on each of the three interventions. Of course we do not know the relative magnitudes of these three costs exactly, but we make assumptions based on circumstantial evidence, and then vary those assumptions to understand how our answers depend on them.

MODEL DETAIL: CONSEQUENCES AND PUBLIC COST OF INTERVENTIONS

Let us now detail the model's first stage. We begin with the implications of spending more money on conventional enforcement—arrests and sentencing. First, we take up the consequences of one additional arrest, i.e., prison time, costs to the person arrested, and reduction in cocaine consumption. Then, we show how much that extra arrest costs the public. These numbers allow an estimate of the consequences of spending an extra million dollars on conventional

---

[2]Boyum (1992) has challenged the assumption that free entry drives long-run profits to zero in drug markets. He points out that in a classic competitive market, competition drives firms that are making negative profits out of business. However, the usual competitive pressures may not exist in drug markets because negative accounting profits that enforce Darwinian selection in conventional markets are not present. Hence, the zero long-run pure profit assumption may not be valid. However, negative accounting profits are not necessary to drive drug dealers out of business. Negative economic profits might make it possible for alternative forms of employment to lure them away from drug dealing.

enforcement. Following the same approach, we then turn to mandatory minimums and treatment of heavy users. Details on sources and calculations can be found in Appendix B.

Arrest and Conventional Sentencing: Consequences

We consider four types of consequences of arrest for suppliers (depicted in Figure 3.8, top): sentences in the form of incarceration and fines, reduction in the demand for cocaine by incarcerated drug sellers who also used cocaine, seizure of cocaine, and seizure of other assets.[3]

Incarceration and Fines. The expected consequences of arrest in terms of incarceration and fines are estimated from data on federal drug cases. We estimate there is an 83.5 percent chance of prosecution given arrest and an 84 percent chance of conviction given prosecution. The anticipated disposition of 100 qualifying arrests is given in Figure 7.2. The numbers in the figure, when divided by 100, thus give the probabilities that a typical qualifying arrest will result in the various dispositions shown. For example, the probability that an arrest will result in a conviction is 0.70 (directly from the figure, or, from the percentages given above, $0.835 \times .84$). The expected consequences of conviction are payment of a \$2,000 fine and an 85.5 percent probability of incarceration for a period of 27 months.[4]

As mentioned above, we are interested in expressing most consequences in dollars. What is the dollar cost to the dealer of spending

---

[3]In many instances, we use data on average consequences—and costs—because data on marginal effects do not exist. As in the analysis reported in Chapter Six, this substitution presumably causes us to underestimate to an unknown degree both the benefits and the costs of mandatory minimums relative to conventional enforcement; the implications for relative cost-effectiveness are thus uncertain.

[4]This 27 months, or, more precisely, 2.26 years, is the average of sentences completed by federal prisoners in 1990 (see Chapter Six). Because mandatory minimums began taking effect in the mid-1980s, the 27-month average may include some sentences imposed under those laws. However, because the cocaine trade and efforts to control it are continuously evolving, we were reluctant to use data that were any older. The effect of using the 1990 exit-year sentence distribution is to confer a small upward bias on the average sentence from conventional enforcement—and thus on its average costs and benefits, relative to those of mandatory minimums. As we find that longer terms result in larger costs relative to benefits, the effect is to underestimate the disadvantage of mandatory minimums relative to conventional enforcement.

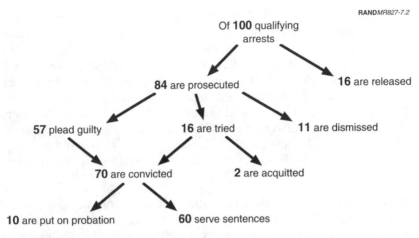

NOTE: 57 + 16 ≠ 70 + 2 because of rounding error; 56.6 + 15.6 = 70.15 + 2.05.

**Figure 7.2—Dispositions of 100 Cocaine Arrests Qualifying
for Mandatory Minimums**

an additional 27 months in prison? In the dynamic analysis, we used $37,500 for yearly cost to a typical dealer. Reuter and Kleiman (1986) estimate somewhat higher numbers for the higher-level dealers arrested by the DEA. They suggest the figures might be $250,000 per year for class 1 violators (as defined by the DEA[5]), $125,000 for class 2, and $75,000 for class 3 or 4. Applying the distribution across classes recorded by the DEA in 1984, they estimate an average of about $102,000 per year of imprisonment for people arrested by the DEA. Adjusting for inflation between 1986 and 1992, this figure becomes $130,600 per year. Typical federal offenders are likely to make more money off drugs than typical dealers in general but less than the higher-level dealers arrested by the DEA. Thus, we use an intermediate value between $37,500 and $130,600 per year, or $85,000 per year.[6]

---

[5]DEA violator classes are defined in terms of factors such as quantity of drug possessed and position in the distribution hierarchy.

[6]If mandatory minimums are applied to people who are not dealers but rather employees of those dealers or couriers for them, the average value of time would be

We recognize, however, that a year of incarceration several years hence would appear less painful than spending a year in prison starting today. That is, just like society in general, drug dealers value present returns more highly than distant ones. In fact, as explained in Chapter Six, they are likely to value them more highly than does society in general. We discount the costs incarceration imposes on dealers by 12 percent. Note that because of this disparity between dealer and social discount rates, longer prison sentences will turn out to be (slightly) less efficient in terms of costs imposed on drug dealers per dollar in prison expenditures incurred by the government.

Reduction in Cocaine Demand. Incarcerating drug dealers affects demand as well as supply because some of those sellers would use drugs if they were free, but results of inmate drug-testing indicate that only a few are able to do so in prison (Harlow, 1992).[7] We estimate that 23.5 percent of people arrested in qualifying arrests are heavy cocaine users and 26.5 percent are light cocaine users.[8] One cannot infer, however, that on average a 27-month term served would avert 0.532 heavy-user-years and 0.600 light-user-years of consumption[9] because, over time, these individuals might have ceased using cocaine even if they were not incarcerated. We use the Everingham and Rydell (1994) model of the evolution of a career of cocaine use to estimate that incapacitating a qualifying drug offender for 27 months would, on average, avert a net present value (discounted at 4 percent) of 0.490 heavy-user-years and 0.499 light-

---

lower. By choosing the $85,000, we are implicitly making the generous assumption that mandatory minimums are hardly ever applied to couriers.

[7]If the number of imprisoned users were significant, the effects on the consumption results would be small, because it turns out that the principal effect of enforcement alternatives on consumption is not direct but mediated by costs (drug and asset seizures and compensation for increased incarceration risk). Also, the effect would be to decrease the estimated reduction in consumption brought about by enforcement, and especially by mandatory minimums, relative to treatment. Thus, to the extent there is any bias, our assumption of negligible prison use favors enforcement, and especially mandatory minimums, relative to treatment.

[8]We use the same probabilities of being a drug user in the static as in the dynamic model. Drug use by federal defendants may be lower than for state and local defendants, but we have no urinalysis data on federal defendants and so cannot be sure. As we show later, the results are not very sensitive to this assumption.

[9]The (approximately) 27-month term is precisely 2.26 years; $0.532 = 2.26 \times .235$, and $0.600 = 2.26 \times .265$.

user-years of cocaine consumption. Since heavy users consume cocaine at eight times the rate that light users do, this is equivalent to averting a net present value of 0.553 heavy-user-years of cocaine demand (0.490 + 0.499/8).

Seizure of Cocaine. The value of drugs seized as a result of a qualifying arrest is estimated from the DEA's STRIDE database.[10] The STRIDE size and price information allow a calculation of the value of drugs involved in any given seizure. The overall average value of drugs seized that could trigger a 5-year mandatory minimum sentence (but not a 10-year sentence) is $16,000, and for 10-year sentences the figure is $332,600. Across all mandatory minimum triggering seizures, the average value is $48,646 (note these are not street values).

Seizure of Other Assets. Data on the value of assets seized per arrest are available for various federal agencies (DEA, FBI, Organized Crime Drug Enforcement (OCDE) Task Forces) and range between $19,000 and $74,000 in assets seized per drug arrest. Much of what is seized is not ultimately retained by the government. Available data suggest that, depending on the agency, something between 25 and 40 percent of what is seized is ultimately forfeited to the government. Hence, we assume that the average value to the suppliers of assets lost per qualifying arrest is $15,000—and that the same value is "recovered" by the government for the purposes of estimating the net cost of making an arrest (for the latter, see below).

Total Consequences. Thus the overall consequences of one qualifying arrest followed by conventional sentencing are as follows:

- A financial penalty of $63,646 worth of drugs and other property lost

- A 70 percent chance of being convicted and paying a further $2,000 fine

---

[10]STRIDE records information on all drug samples analyzed by DEA laboratories. In particular, it includes information on the date, size, location, and nature of all seizures; this information plus price is available for purchase observations. See Frank (1987) for details.

- A 60 percent chance of being incarcerated for an expected term of 27 months, which avoids an average of 0.553 heavy-user-years of cocaine consumption.

Total cost imposed on the dealer is thus $63,600 + 0.70($2,000) + 0.60($85,000 × 27/12, discounted to present value), or approximately $167,000.

Arrest and Conventional Sentencing: Public Cost

The Office of National Drug Control Policy (ONDCP) (1992, pp. 90, 94) reports that the DEA, with an investigations budget of $562.9 million in 1992, made 19,562 arrests[11] and was associated with another 10,003,[12] for a cost of $19,000–$29,000 per arrest. Similarly, the FBI (ONDCP, 1992, p. 95) spent $201 million completing 8,100 investigations (about $25,000 per investigation—though no data are available on arrests per investigation). The Bureau of Alcohol, Tobacco and Firearms (ONDCP, 1992, p. 168) had an investigations budget of $128.5 million and recommended 7,072 suspects for prosecution, or about $18,000 per suspect. From these data, we infer a very round figure of $20,000 investigation cost per qualifying federal arrest.[13]

From data reported by Greenwood et al. (1994) for average criminal justice processing costs in 1993, we calculate $1,262 in adjudication costs per arrest in 1992, and $3,880 in court costs per trial in 1992, or $605 per arrest ($3,880 × 15.6 trials/100 arrests).[14] For the public cost

---

[11]Includes DEA initiated arrests, DEA cooperative arrests, and DEA/OCDE arrests.

[12]Includes federal referral arrests and state and local task force arrests.

[13]This is higher than the typical arrest cost across all jurisdictions. In 1991, for example, state and local government spent $4.223 billion and federal enforcement agencies spent $1.288 billion (ONDCP, 1993) making 1,010,000 arrests (FBI, 1992), or $5,500 per arrest.

[14]These data derived from Greenwood et al. (1994) are for state and local costs (specifically, California). We use the Greenwood data because we believe them to be more precise than analogous federal data and because we also use them in the dynamic analysis. The comparison between the two analyses is more interesting if as much as possible of the difference between them is in the level of offenders considered. Federal costs are probably somewhat higher, but not much.

The figure of $1,262 in adjudication costs per arrest is consistent with a 1991 estimate of $1.3 billion in prosecution and legal service costs, public-defense costs, and costs of

of a cell-year of incarceration, we use the estimate of $24,972 from Chapter Six.

The government cost incurred for a 27-month term served is not just 2.26 times this figure because not all of the expenses have to be paid in the first year, and expenses paid in subsequent years are worth less in present value. The net present value of corrections costs associated with a 27-month sentence, discounted monthly at a real annual social discount rate of 4 percent, is $54,130. The net present value of corrections costs associated with a qualifying arrest is then 0.60 times that number, or $32,480.

From these costs must be subtracted the values of fines collected and nondrug assets seized and forfeited per qualifying arrest. As discussed in the previous subsection, these are, respectively, $1,403 ($2,000 per conviction × 70.15 convictions per 100 arrests) and $15,000.

Thus the total cost to the government per qualifying arrest with conventional sentencing is

$20,000	arrest
$1,262	adjudication cost per arrest
$605	trial cost per arrest
$32,480	expected net present value of corrections cost
($1,403)	expected values of fines collected
($15,000)	value of nondrug assets seized and forfeited
$37,944	Total

---

other criminal justice activities, divided by 1,010,000 drug arrests in 1991 (FBI, 1992). (The $1.3 billion figure is a combination of state and local costs from ONDCP (1993) and federal data from ONDCP (1992); it assumes that two-thirds of federal expenditures were associated with domestic enforcement.) The comparable estimate for court costs is $659 million divided by (15.6 trials/100 arrests) × 1,010,000 arrests = 157,000 trials, or about $4,200 per trial, which is reasonably close to the estimate derived from Greenwood et al. (1994).

By spending $1 million, one could make 26.35 more qualifying arrests with conventional sentencing. Doing so would

- impose 26.35 × ($63,646 + $1,403) = $1,714,000 in financial costs on suppliers (fines, lost assets, plus lost drugs)

- put 16 drug dealers behind bars for 27.2 months each, bringing total costs imposed on dealers to $4.39 million, and, thereby

- avert a net present value of 9 heavy-user-years (16 dealers × 0.553 heavy-user-years/dealer) of cocaine demand.

Mandatory Minimums: Consequences and Costs

To estimate the consequences and costs of imposing mandatory minimum sentences, we follow a simple two-step process. First, we repeat the calculations just described with parameter values reflecting what would happen with longer sentences. Then we subtract the costs and consequences with current sentences from the results of these calculations to find the incremental costs and consequences of extending sentences.

Our estimates of the costs and consequences of arrest and sentencing with mandatory minimum sentences use the same basic data and differ in only three respects from conventional sentencing. The first and by far the most important difference is that longer sentences are imposed and a larger fraction of those sentences are served. Specifically, we assume, as we did in Chapter Six, that two-thirds of the cases trigger 5-year mandatory sentences and one-third trigger 10-year sentences, for an average sentence of 6.7 years. We assume that every offender convicted is incarcerated and that on average 100 percent of this minimum sentence is served.

Second, these longer sentences lead to greater reductions in cocaine demand per person sentenced. With the Everingham and Rydell (1994) model, we estimate that, on average, a 6.7-year sentence would avert 1.360 heavy-user-years of cocaine consumption.

Third, presumably when faced with an expected sentence given conviction that is nearly seven years instead of a little over two years if convicted, more defendants will demand a trial. Greenwood et al. (1994), in modeling California's "Three Strikes and You're Out" law, assumed the fraction of felony cases going to trial doubled for second- and third-strike cases. Here the change in expected sentence length is less dramatic, so we use a figure of 30 percent of prosecuted mandatory minimum drug cases going to trial, i.e., 25 out of 84, for an increase in the trial rate of approximately 60 percent. (We assume no change in the rate of dismissal, so the rate of guilty pleas drops from 68 percent to 56 percent, or from 57 pleas to 47 for every 84 prosecutions or every 100 arrests.)[15] This increases the average trial cost per arrest from $605 to $973 and decreases the probability of conviction given arrest from 70.15 percent to 68.90 percent.[16]

With longer sentences and a greater chance of trial, the government cost per arrest is increased from $37,944 to $106,729. So spending $1 million allows one to make 9.4 qualifying arrests. Doing so would impose $468,865 in financial costs on suppliers, put at least six offenders behind bars for close to seven years each and, thereby, avert a net present value of 8.8 heavy-user-years of cocaine consumption.

Now consider the consequences of imposing mandatory minimum sentences on offenders who have already been arrested, but otherwise would have been prosecuted under conventional sentencing. The cost per arrestee of doing so is $68,785 ($106,729 – $37,944). Dividing that number into $1 million indicates that extending sentences could be applied to perhaps 15 qualifying arrests. The consequence would be that the 10 individuals convicted and incarcerated would serve an expected sentence of 80 not 27.2 months, for an additional cost imposed on the average individual arrested of $169,000 or a total additional cost of $2.45 million. This would avert an additional net present value per qualifying arrest of 0.61 heavy-user-year of consumption,[17] or, when multiplied by the expected

---

[15]Note, in neither the Greenwood study nor this one are the overall results very sensitive to this change in trial rate.

[16]As mentioned in Chapter Two, there may be an increase in plea bargains struck with defendants afraid of losing at trial. If so, that would reduce the small effects postulated here.

[17](1.36 heavy-user-years/prisoner × .69 prisoner/arrest with the previous alternative) – (0.55 heavy-user-year/prisoner × .60 prisoner/arrest with conventional enforcement.)

14.5 qualifying arrests, a total of 8.8 heavy-user-years of consumption averted. (Of course, there is no additional financial cost for suppliers in terms of forfeited drugs and assets because the number of arrests is not changed, and the difference in expected fines due to the difference in expected convictions is small.)

Treating Heavy Drug Users: Consequences and Costs

It was estimated in Chapter Six that spending $1 million on treatment would avert a net present value of 103.6 kilograms of cocaine consumption, which is 0.0356 percent of the estimated 291 metric tons consumed annually. Below, we derive a formula to convert a 1 percent change in demand into the resulting percentage change in the quantity consumed.[18] Applying the formula in reverse allows us to calculate the percentage change in demand generated by spending $1 million more treating heavy cocaine users. The result is a reduction of 639 heavy-user-years of demand.

MODEL DETAIL: EFFECTS ON THE MARKET

We now show how we translate the changes in enforcement-related costs and demand reductions estimated above into movements in the cocaine-market supply and demand curves. We also describe how we evaluate the implications of those movements for cocaine price and consumption and total spending on cocaine.

Demand and Supply Curves

A market model requires expressions for the demand curve and supply curve. We develop these as follows.

Demand. The overall shape of the demand curve for cocaine is not known, but for modest departures from the current market equilibrium a linear approximation is sufficient and can be written:

---

[18]The two percentage changes are the same only if the price elasticity of the quantity supplied is infinite, i.e., if the price is the same regardless of the amount supplied. In the standard graph of market price versus quantity, the first change represents a leftward or rightward shift in the demand curve; the second change, movement along a stationary demand curve.

$$Q_D(P) = Q_0\left(1 + \eta\left(\frac{P}{P_0} - 1\right)\right) ,$$

where

P = market clearing price,

$Q_D(P)$ = quantity consumed at a market price of P,

P_0 = market price in initial equilibrium,

Q_0 = market clearing quantity in initial equilibrium, and

η = the elasticity of demand.

Changes in demand manifest as changes in Q_0. For example, if the demand grew by 5 percent, then the demand curve would be the same as above with Q_0 replaced by 1.05 Q_0.

Supply. A more complicated model of the supply curve is needed. As mentioned above, the supply model we utilize here is based on Reuter and Kleiman's (1986) "risks-and-prices" approach, which postulates that, because of low barriers to entry, free entry will drive long-run pure economic profits to zero. In that case, the supply curve can be found by estimating costs as a function of the quantity sold.

One can imagine three dominant categories of costs associated with supplying drugs:

- Unit costs proportional to the quantity of drugs sold (e.g., normal business costs such as labor, transportation, packaging, and compensation for hours worked).

- Market costs proportional to the value of drugs sold (e.g., compensation for the risks of fraud, robbery, injury, and death at the hands of other market participants).

- Market costs proportional to enforcement spending (compensation for the risks of arrest, incarceration, and the impact of a felony conviction on future licit earnings potential).

The assumption made here about normal business costs is the same one that underlies the common, albeit very simple, model of a linear supply curve for conventional products (like shirts and shoes). A linear supply curve in a competitive market implies that the unit price asked by suppliers to compensate them for their production costs varies linearly with the total quantity sold.

The model for drug supply considered here differs from that elementary model in that it includes two other categories of cost, which are negligible or nonexistent for suppliers of most licit products. First, the drug supply industry collectively incurs costs proportional to the dollar value of the drugs sold because drug suppliers cannot rely on the police for protection against robbery or on the courts for protection from fraud. Neither can drug dealers use the courts to collect from customers who default. As a result, the incidence of robbery, fraud, and default in illicit markets is high. All of these types of disputes lead to violence, and some of drug dealers' accounting profits can be viewed as compensation for the financial and physical risks associated with these disputes.

Occasionally these disputes are driven by the quantity of the drug itself, e.g. when an addict robs a dealer to obtain a "fix." More often they are driven by the value of the drug. For a drug dealer's courier, the temptation to abscond depends on the value of what he or she is carrying, not the weight. When a drug dealer contemplates shooting another dealer to take over that dealer's "turf," it is the dollar value of the potential increase in sales, not the quantity measured in kilograms, that is balanced against the risks of exercising violence. Much of the violence associated with the drug trade and, hence, the amount of drug dealers' revenues that can be viewed as compensation for that violence is modeled here as being proportional to the dollar value of the cocaine sales.

The second prominent category of costs for drug dealers that is largely absent for licit enterprises is compensation for the risks of arrest and associated consequences. We assume these costs are linear in enforcement spending.

Note, the total costs of supplying drugs are not linear in enforcement spending because of what Reuter (1983) refers to as the "structural consequences of product illegality." That is, the fact of illegality coupled with a modicum of enforcement would greatly increase costs relative to no enforcement whatsoever because it would force dealers to operate at least somewhat covertly (e.g., not advertise or maintain a fixed place of business). However, in this model those costs are captured in the other two terms. The costs associated with enforcement here (the third term) are only those associated with the consequences discussed above: the risk of arrest, incarceration, fines, seizures of drugs, and seizure of other assets.

In addition, there are some other, smaller, costs that fit into these three categories. For example, if drug dealers view their activities as "investing" money in buying drugs from their supplier and expect to obtain a particular "return" on investment, then this component of compensation will be proportional to the dollar value of the market. (See Boyum, 1992.) Likewise, if cocaine dealers pay employees (e.g., lookouts or touters) by giving them a fraction of the cocaine sold, then the cost of those wages will be proportional to the value of cocaine sold.

At any rate, with this division of dealers' costs and since, according to the risks-and-prices framework, total revenues equal the sum of all costs, we can write:

$$P_s(Q)Q = (c + dQ)Q + \gamma(PQ) + E$$

where

$P_s(Q)$ = supply curve,

Q = market clearing quantity,

$c + dQ$ = regular business costs per unit sold,

γ = fraction of supplier costs that are proportional to value of drugs sold, and

E = enforcement (denominated in dollars of costs imposed on suppliers).

An expression for the industry supply curve can be obtained by solving for $P_s(Q)$.

Implications for Consumption, Price, and Spending

We now equate the demand and supply curves, deriving parameters that express the relations between changes in enforcement or demand and changes in consumption, price, and spending. We then estimate those parameters.

Equating Demand and Supply. If we invert the demand curve (to express price as a function of quantity) and set it equal to the supply curve (i.e., find their point of intersection) we obtain the market clearing quantity consumed and price and, thus, total spending on the drug.[19] By taking derivatives, we can find the rate of change of each of these quantities with respect to changes in enforcement spending or the demand for cocaine. The details are described in Appendix C. Table 7.1 gives these results expressed in terms of five parameters:

η =   the elasticity of demand;

$\alpha_0 = \dfrac{cQ_0}{P_0 Q_0}$ these two parameters together represent the fraction of cocaine sales revenue in the original equilibrium that compensates dealers for the "normal business costs" associated with distributing cocaine;

$\alpha_1 = \dfrac{dQ_0^2}{P_0 Q_0}$

γ =   the fraction of cocaine sales revenue that compensates dealers for costs that are proportional to the value of cocaine sales;[20] and

$\beta = \dfrac{E_0}{Q_0 P_0} =$ the fraction of cocaine sales revenue in the original equilibrium that compensates dealers for the costs of arrest, incarceration, fines, cocaine seizures, and asset seizures.

---

[19]In the original equilibrium (prior to program initiation), these are 291 metric tons, $129 per pure gram, and $37.6 billion, respectively (Rydell and Everingham, 1994).

[20]Note that the other parameters are defined in terms of the original equilibrium. The value of γ does not change with the equilibrium, but of course its value is then always the same as it is in the original equilibrium.

Note that, by definition, $\alpha_0 + \alpha_1 + \gamma + \beta = 1$.

Thus, from Table 7.1, the percentage change in consumption brought about by a 1 percent increase in the costs enforcement imposes on dealers is $\beta\eta/[1 - \gamma + (\beta - \alpha_1)\eta]$. Note: No market equilibrium exists unless the denominator in these expressions, $[1 - \gamma + (\beta - \alpha_1)\eta]$, is greater than zero.

Once estimated, these parameters allow us to calculate the cocaine consumption, price, and spending implications of a $1 million increase in program costs. Doing so requires expressing the consequences of that cost increase in terms of changes in parameters. The same approach can be used to test the sensitivity of the results to variations in parameters and other input values. Thus, variation in the fraction of dealers who are heavy users changes the drop in cocaine consumption per year of imprisonment. That changes the 1 percent drop in demand assumed in the last column of Table 7.1 and the quotients in that column proportionately. Changing the arrest cost alters the number of additional arrests per million dollars spent and thus the percentage changes in both enforcement and demand.

Estimating Parameters. The parameters listed above—η, α_0, α_1, β, and γ—are not known, and they can only be estimated roughly. Hence, we thoroughly analyze the sensitivity of our results to their values.

Table 7.1

How Market Quantities Respond When Enforcement or Demand Changes

Percentage Change in	If There Is a	
	1% Increase in Costs That Enforcement Imposes on Dealers	1% Increase in Demand
Consumption =	$\dfrac{\beta\eta}{1 - \gamma + (\beta - \alpha_1)\eta}$	$\dfrac{1 - \gamma}{1 - \gamma + (\beta - \alpha_1)\eta}$
Price =	$\dfrac{\beta}{1 - \gamma + (\beta - \alpha_1)\eta}$	$\dfrac{\alpha_1 - \beta}{1 - \gamma + (\beta - \alpha_1)\eta}$
Spending =	$\dfrac{\beta(1 + \eta)}{1 - \gamma + (\beta - \alpha_1)\eta}$	$\dfrac{1 - \gamma - (\beta - \alpha_1)}{1 - \gamma + (\beta - \alpha_1)\eta}$

As discussed in Chapter Six, the best available current evidence suggests that, for cocaine, η is about -1. As for the other three parameters, the cost structure of the drug dealing "industry" is, of course, not known. Fortunately our results are fairly robust with respect to assumptions about these three parameters, but some base case is needed.

First, we assume that $\alpha_1 = 0$. This is equivalent to assuming that none of the normal factors of production in drug distribution (e.g., land and farmers in South America, smugglers, supply of labor willing to sell drugs within the United States, etc.) is in such short supply that those factors could bid up their compensation if the market expanded. This is a recognition that few technical skills are required at any level of drug production and distribution and that barriers to entry are low.

To the extent that α_1 is in fact greater than 0, this assumption would inflate our estimates of the cocaine-consumption-reducing ability of both imposing costs on dealers and reducing demand. Hence, if this assumption is in error, it will make all three programs seem better than they are, and by the same proportions. The assumption likewise exaggerates the impact that imposing costs on dealers has on both the market price and users' spending on cocaine; the assumption has an ambiguous effect on estimates of demand reduction's impact on market price and user spending.

As to the other parameters, Reuter, MacCoun, and Murphy (1990) give the most detailed information about the economics of cocaine selling. It applies only to street selling, but inferences can be drawn about the values of α_0, β, and γ if one assumes these results can be applied to the entire distribution system. Such an assumption is obviously a stretch, but it is at least somewhat reassuring that most of the value added in drug distribution comes at the lower levels of the distribution network.

Reuter, MacCoun, and Murphy (p. ix) report that most sales are made by the 37 percent of sellers who work daily (mean gross monthly income of $6,800; mean net monthly income $3,600) and the 40 percent who sell on two or more days per week (mean monthly gross and net incomes of $2,510 and $1,200, respectively). Within this group, the average seller has a gross and net annual income of $54,840 and $28,200, respectively. "Net income subtracts all costs the respondents could identify, including drugs purchased for resale" (p. vii). These subtracted costs ($26,640) are probably typical costs of doing business, suggesting that α_0 is at least 0.49.

Reuter, MacCoun, and Murphy (p. xii) also report that dealers working at least two days a week incur a 1.4 percent annual risk of death and a 7 percent annual risk of injury because of their dealing. Reuter, MacCoun, and Murphy judge that together these risks warrant compensation of $12,600 per year, suggesting that γ is at least 0.23.   One way to check whether Reuter, MacCoun, and Murphy's figures are sensible for the nation as a whole is to see what they imply for how drug dealers value risk of death. Their study reports that $10,500 of the $12,600 risk compensation was associated with the risk of death. Our appendix D estimates that roughly 3,500 homicides per year in the United States are related to cocaine selling. Not all of those victims are drug dealers, but suppose that 3,000 were. That figure of 3,000 drug dealers being killed could be reconciled with the $10,500 figure if the average drug dealer values his or her life at $2.4 million.[21]   Or, since drug dealers face a risk of death, not certain death, it would be more accurate to say Reuter, MacCoun, and Murphy's estimates for Washington, D.C., seem consistent with national data on homicides if the average drug dealer would demand $24,000 to compensate him or her for an additional 1 percent risk of being killed.

The parameter γ should reflect all of the costs that are proportional to the dollar value of the drugs sold. The dominant such costs are related to violence, but another cost is any wages paid in kind, that is, in the form of drugs. Suppose a lookout or other assistant is paid a rock of cocaine for assisting with the sale of a gram to someone else. Then the effective cost of the assistant's wage to the drug dealer increases with the price of the drug and is proportional to the value of the drugs sold. Rhodes et al. (1995) estimate that as much as 10 percent of retail sales take the form of payment in kind for labor, suggesting that γ is somewhat greater than 0.23.

---

[21]Because $2.4M \times 3,000 \times (\$12.6K/\$10.5K)/\$37.6B = 0.23$.

Now let us turn to β, the fraction of cocaine sales revenue compensating dealers for enforcement-related costs. Reuter, MacCoun, and Murphy (1990) estimate that even if dealers working at least two days a week demanded only $20,000 in monetary compensation per additional expected year of incarceration, they would still need $9,000 per year of selling on the street to compensate them for the risks of incarceration. This suggests that β is at least $9,000/$54,840 = 0.164.

However, suppose that about 200,000 people incarcerated for drug law violations in the United States sold cocaine, that they demand an average of $37,500 per year (Kleiman, 1992) as compensation for their time, and that the cocaine market is worth $37.6 billion (Rydell and Everingham, 1994).[22] These figures suggest that β is at least $(200,000 \times 37,500)/37,600,000,000 = 0.20$. We say "at least" because a dealer would presumably require an amount beyond the income lost to compensate him or her for time spent incarcerated.

We take as base-case estimates that $\alpha_0 = 55$ percent, $\alpha_1 = 0$ percent, $\gamma = 25$ percent, and $\beta = 20$ percent but perform sensitivity analyses around these parameter values. These values reflect the estimates derived above and the requirement that they sum to 1.

To review, the five key parameters of the market model are shown in Table 7.2.

COST-EFFECTIVENESS AT REDUCING CONSUMPTION AND SPENDING

Base Case

Table 7.3 summarizes the results of spending $1 million on each of three programs: (1) expanding conventional arrest, prosecution, and

---

[22]Note that the compensation rates in this paragraph and the preceding are lower than the value given above of $85,000, because these rates are for all dealers; we use these values for our current purposes because we are considering the entire market. We use the higher number elsewhere because it is more relevant to our focus on defendants in federal prosecutions, who are typically higher-level dealers and are likely to demand higher rates of compensation.

Table 7.2

Values of Key Parameters

Symbol	Base Value	Definition
η	−1.0	Elasticity of demand for cocaine
α_0 $+ \alpha_1$	0.55 0	Fraction of cocaine sales revenue that compensates dealers for costs proportional to the quantity sold
γ	0.25	Fraction of cocaine sales revenue that compensates dealers for costs proportional to value of cocaine sales
β	0.20	Fraction of cocaine sales revenue that compensates dealers for the costs of arrest, incarceration, fines, cocaine seizures, and asset seizures

sentencing of high-level offenders, (2) prosecuting under mandatory minimum laws some federal drug defendants, who would otherwise have been prosecuted under conventional sentencing laws, and (3) treating heavy users. These results are discussed in Chapter Three. We note here only that the $9.8 million in cocaine sales prevented by a $1 million investment in treatment is not far from the $8.6 million projected by the methods used in Chapter Six. The disparity results from a difference in slope between the supply curves estimated with the different modeling approaches.

Sensitivity Analysis

Most single-variable, and some dual-variable, sensitivity analyses are reported in Chapter Three. We undertake here three additional sensitivity analyses. All three affirm the conclusion of the earlier sensitivity analysis: The primary results are not very sensitive to uncertainty about parameter values.

In the first sensitivity analysis, we extend the single-variable analysis to the results for reducing cocaine expenditures. We limit ourselves to presenting the results of varying the assumed elasticity of demand;

Table 7.3

Effects of Spending an Additional $1 Million on Various Cocaine Control Programs at the Federal Level: Base-Case Assumptions

Outcome	Program		
	Conventional Enforcement	Mandatory Minimums	Treating Heavy Users
Intermediate Effects			
Net government cost per person affected	$37,944	$68,785	$1,740
People affected	26.35	14.54	574.71
Cost imposed on dealers per person affected	$166,755	$168,822	$0
Total costs imposed	$4.39 million	$2.45 million	$0
Demand averted per person affected	0.332 heavy-user-yr	0.605 heavy-user-yr	1.112 heavy-user-yr
Demand averted	8.74 heavy-user-yr	8.80 heavy-user-yr	638.80 heavy-user-yr
Market Outcomes			
Change in consumption (Q)	−63.3 kg	−36.0 kg	−103.6 kg
Change in market price (P)	$0.0276/gram	$0.0155/gram	$0.0123/gram
Change in spending (PQ)	−$134,400	−$135,100	−$9,815,800

varying other inputs do not result in interesting changes in cocaine revenues. The elasticity results are reported in Figure 7.3 in terms of cocaine spending reduced per million program dollars.

As the elasticity of demand falls below −1.0 (moves to the right on the horizontal axis), the ratio of the cost-effectiveness of treatment to that of conventional enforcement drops, falling from 73:1 to 2.4:1 when the elasticity reaches −1.5. Over the same range, treatment's advantage over mandatory minimums drops from 73:1 to about 4:1. Conventional enforcement improves relative to mandatory minimums, from parity to 1.7:1. The enforcement alternatives look somewhat better on the right-hand side of the graph, where the

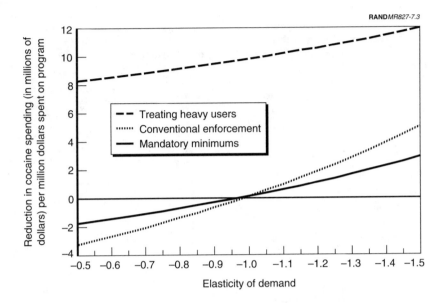

**Figure 7.3—How Cocaine Control Programs Affect Spending on Cocaine:
Sensitivity to Elasticity of Demand**

quantity consumed (*Q*) drops by larger percentages than the price
(*P*) increases; thus, the total revenue (*PQ*) falls. But as the elasticity
decreases in absolute terms (moves to the left on the graph), the
lower responsiveness of quantities consumed to price changes results in increasing total revenue, and enforcement alternatives look
progressively worse.

In the second sensitivity analysis, we extend the analysis to the cost
allocation parameters. For convenience, we repeat the single-variable analysis of Table 3.6 in Table 7.4, this time including the cost
allocation parameters α_0, β, and γ. As the table shows, cocaine consumption is not as sensitive to variations in the model parameters
relating to allocation of costs (α_0, β, and γ) as they are to some of the
other input variables. However, those parameters could be esti-
mated only very roughly, and α_0 and especially γ do appear to influence in some degree the cost-effectiveness of treatment relative to

Table 7.4

How Between-Program Ratios for Cost-Effectiveness at Reducing Cocaine Consumption Vary with Input Variable Values

Input Variable	Values	Cost-Effectiveness Relative to That of Mandatory Minimums for Federal Defendants	
		Treatment	Federal-Level Conventional Enforcement
Elasticity of demand	−1 (base value)	2.9	1.8
	−0.5	5.5	1.7
	−1.5	1.9	1.8
Cost imposed on dealers per year in prison	$85,000 (base value)	2.9	1.8
	$37,500	6.2	2.5
	$130,000	1.9	1.5
Police cost per arrest	$20,000 (base value)	2.9	1.8
	$10,000	2.9	2.4
	$30,000	2.9	1.4
α_0 = fraction of selling costs proportional to quantity	0.55 (base value)	2.9	1.8
	0.25 (β=0.35;γ=0.4)	2.3	1.8
	0.85 (β=0.05;γ=0.1)	3.4	1.8
β = fraction of Selling costs proportional to enforcement	0.20 (base value)	2.9	1.8
	0.05 (α_0=0.625; γ=0.325)	2.6	1.8
	0.35 (α_0=0.475; γ=0.175)	3.2	1.8
γ = fraction of selling costs proportional to value of market	0.25 (base value)	2.9	1.8
	0.05 (α_0=0.65;β=0.3)	3.6	1.8
	0.45 (α_0=0.45;β=0.1)	2.1	1.8
Fraction of dealers who are heavy users	23.5% (base value)	2.9	1.8
	0%	3.0	1.8
	47%	2.8	1.7
Rate at which dealers discount future events	0.12 (base value)	2.9	1.8
	0.04	2.1	1.4
	0.06	2.3	1.4
	0.18	3.6	2.1
	0.30	5.4	3.0
Value of drugs seized per arrest	$48,646 (base value)	2.9	1.8
	$25,000	2.9	1.5
	$100,000	2.9	2.3

Table 7.4—continued

| Input Variable | Values | Cost-Effectiveness Relative to That of Mandatory Minimums for Federal Defendants | |
		Treatment	Federal-Level Conventional Enforcement
Value of other	$15,000 (base value)	2.9	1.8
assets forfeited	$7,500	2.9	1.4
per arrest	$30,000	2.9	3.2
Average sentence	80 months (base value)	2.9	1.8
with mandatory	60 months	2.7	1.7
minimum	120 months	3.2	2.0
Fraction of	30% (base value)	2.9	1.8
arrests leading	17%	2.9	1.7
to trial for mandatory	60%	2.9	1.8
min. sentences			

the enforcement alternatives. We are thus also interested in how the results depend on simultaneous variation of these parameters and on the resulting interaction between them.

Recall that $\beta = 1 - \alpha_0 - \gamma$ while $\alpha_1 = 0$ as is assumed here. Since the parameters are interdependent and at least two must be varied simultaneously, the analysis in Table 7.4 seeks to minimize the effect of a single-parameter test on the two untested parameters by moving both in the opposite direction. Here, we hold one constant and vary two others by equal amounts in opposite directions. In Table 7.5, we hold α_0 constant down the columns, while γ and β are varied. We hold γ constant across the rows, while α_0 and β are varied.

Several patterns are apparent from Table 7.5. To begin, the efficacy of both enforcement programs varies by less than 5 percent as γ (and β) varies from 0 to .9, with constant α_0. Furthermore, the ratio of these two programs' effectiveness is almost invariant with respect to changes in all three parameters. Conventional enforcement's effectiveness is always between 1.74 and 1.80 times that of extending sentences for any set of parameter values shown in the table.

Table 7.5

Sensitivity of Cocaine Consumption Results to Simultaneous Variation of Cost Allocation Parameters

γ	Kilograms of Consumption Averted Per Million-Dollar Program Expenditure									
	$\alpha_0=.1$	$\alpha_0=.2$	$\alpha_0=.3$	$\alpha_0=.4$	$\alpha_0=.5$	$\alpha_0=.6$	$\alpha_0=.7$	$\alpha_0=.8$	$\alpha_0=.9$	$\alpha_0=1$
Program: treating heavy users										
0.9	76.0									
0.8	151.9	76.0								
0.7	227.9	114.0	76.0							
0.6	303.9	151.9	101.3	76.0						
0.5	379.9	189.9	126.6	95.0	76.0					
0.4	455.8	227.9	151.9	114.0	91.2	76.0				
0.3	531.8	265.9	177.3	133.0	106.4	88.6	76.0			
0.2	607.8	303.9	202.6	151.9	121.6	101.3	86.8	76.0		
0.1	683.8	341.9	227.9	170.9	136.8	114.0	97.7	85.5	76.0	
0	759.7	379.9	253.2	189.9	151.9	126.6	108.5	95.0	84.4	76.0
Program: conventional enforcement										
0.9	341.2									
0.8	342.2	171.1								
0.7	343.3	171.6	114.4							
0.6	344.3	172.2	114.8	86.1						
0.5	345.4	172.7	115.1	86.3	69.1					
0.4	346.4	173.2	115.5	86.6	69.3	57.7				
0.3	347.4	173.7	115.8	86.9	69.5	57.9	49.6			
0.2	348.5	174.2	116.2	87.1	69.7	58.1	49.8	43.6		
0.1	349.5	174.8	116.5	87.4	69.9	58.3	49.9	43.7	38.8	
0	350.6	175.3	116.9	87.6	70.1	58.4	50.1	43.8	39.0	35.1
Program: mandatory minimums										
0.9	191.0									
0.8	192.1	96.0								
0.7	193.1	96.6	64.4							
0.6	194.1	97.1	64.7	48.5						
0.5	195.2	97.6	65.1	48.8	39.0					
0.4	196.2	98.1	65.4	49.1	39.2	32.7				
0.3	197.3	98.6	65.8	49.3	39.5	32.9	28.2			
0.2	198.3	99.2	66.1	49.6	39.7	33.1	28.3	24.8		
0.1	199.4	99.7	66.5	49.8	39.9	33.2	28.5	24.9	22.2	
0	200.4	100.2	66.8	50.1	40.1	33.4	28.6	25.1	22.3	20.0

NOTES: For definition of parameters, see Table 7.2.

Base case: $\alpha_0 = .55$, $\gamma = .25$, $\beta = .2$.

Treatment's effectiveness relative to that of either enforcement program depends only on γ. It is invariant with respect to α_0 (and hence β) for any fixed γ. Since conventional enforcement is always more effective than extending sentences for all combinations of parameter values shown in the table, the programs' effectiveness rankings are simply dependent on γ as shown in Table 7.6. Given the base-case assumption that γ is only 0.25, the implication of Table 7.6 is that the program rankings are not very sensitive to the values of the parameters.

In the third sensitivity analysis, we investigated the sensitivity of our results to simultaneous variation in multiple parameters through Monte Carlo simulation. Uncertainty concerning eight of the most important parameters was described using elementary probability distributions (Table 7.7). Values of these random variables were drawn independently and used to evaluate the model 16,000 times.

Overall the results (shown in Table 7.8) indicated that the conclusions about *relative* cost-effectiveness drawn above are very robust with respect to uncertainty in the parameters. There is more uncertainty with respect to the *absolute* estimates of cost-effectiveness.

For example, over 16,000 runs, the average estimate of extending sentences' ability to reduce cocaine use was 39 kilograms per million program dollars spent, and for 90 percent of the simulation runs, the

Table 7.6

Ranking of Program Cost-Effectiveness as a Function of γ

Range of γ	Most Effective Program	Second-Most-Effective Program	Least Effective Program
$\gamma < 0.546$	Treatment	Conventional enforcement	Extending sentences
$0.546 < \gamma < 0.746$	Conventional enforcement	Treatment	Extending sentences
$\gamma > 0.746$	Conventional enforcement	Extending sentences	Treatment

Table 7.7

Monte Carlo Sensitivity Analysis: Distributions for Eight Inputs Varied

Parameter	Lower Bound	Mode	Upper Bound
Triangle distribution			
Elasticity of demand	–0.5	–1	–1.5
Value of dealer's time	$37,500	$85,000	$130,000
Police cost per arrest	$10,000	$20,000	$30,000
Value of drugs seized			
per arrest	$25,000	$48,646	$100,000
Value of other assets			
forfeited per arrest	$7,500	$15,000	$30,000
α_0	0.25	0.55	0.85
Uniform distribution			
Dealers' discount rate	6.0%		18.0%
β	Max(0.05, $(1-\alpha)/9$)		Min(0.35, $7 \times (1-\alpha)/9$)

NOTE: The triangle distribution is a continuous probability density function that is zero below its lower bound, rises linearly to a peak at its mode, and decreases linearly to zero at its upper bound. The parameter β was not modeled this way because parameters α_0, β, and γ are related; they sum to unity. Instead β was modeled as equally likely to take on any value between its lower and upper bounds. As for the other parameters, the bounds for β were taken to be those in the one-way sensitivity analysis. Those bounds are 0.05 and 0.35, or, stated in terms of β's relation to α in that analysis, $(1-\alpha)/9$ and $7(1-\alpha)/9$. Taking the less extreme of the two upper bounds ensures that γ is not close to zero or negative, as would be the case if α were 0.85 and β 0.35. To be consistent, we also take the less extreme of the two lower bounds.

estimated impact was between 17 and 75 kilograms. For conventional enforcement the average was 81 kilograms, and 90 percent of the estimates fell between 35 and 158 kilograms. For treatment, the average was 111 kilograms, with 90 percent falling between 90 and 147 kilograms.

These ranges overlap, but generally when a parameter is shifted in such a way that one program appears absolutely more cost-effective, the other two programs are affected similarly. This is especially true for the two enforcement programs. Hence, in only two of the 16,000 trials was extending sentences more effective than was conventional enforcement at reducing cocaine use. Similarly, long sentences were more effective than treating heavy cocaine users in only seven of the 16,000 runs, and in no instance were long sentences the most effec-

Table 7.8

**How Cost-Effectiveness at Reducing Cocaine Consumption Varies with
Simultaneous Random Variation in Input Values**

	Decrease in Quantity Consumed (kg) Per Additional Million Dollars			Ratio of Consumption Effects	
	Mandatory Minimums	Conventional Enforcement	Treating heavy users	Conv. Enf. vs. Man. Min.	Treatment vs. Man. Min.
Average	39.19	81.14	110.81	2.14	3.32
Variance	373.71	1672.48	384.63	0.37	1.67
Min, max, and percentiles					
Min	7.05	14.86	81.52	0.99	0.91
1%	12.93	26.92	86.03	1.21	1.35
5%	16.91	35.22	89.61	1.37	1.70
25%	25.86	53.46	97.47	1.71	2.39
50%	35.05	71.96	106.27	2.03	3.07
75%	47.66	98.06	118.84	2.45	3.98
95%	75.06	157.83	147.25	3.29	5.79
99%	106.10	224.31	181.35	4.07	7.36
Max	235.11	547.70	352.11	7.32	12.30

tive program. (Treatment beat conventional enforcement in 86 percent of the trials.)

COST-EFFECTIVENESS AT REDUCING CRIME

We do not reproduce here the results from Chapter Four, but we present in Table 7.9 a Monte Carlo sensitivity analysis of those results undertaken by the same methods as those discussed above. The analysis demonstrates that treatment's enormous edge in cost-effectiveness at reducing crime is not threatened by uncertainty in parameter values. Treatment was superior to mandatory minimum sentences in every trial and was superior to conventional enforcement in all but 26 of the trials (i.e., in 99.8 percent of the trials). Mandatory minimum sentences had a more beneficial impact on crime than did conventional enforcement in 25 percent of the trials (4,013 of 16,000). However, in most of those cases the elasticity of demand was low, so when enforcement drove up cocaine

Table 7.9

How Cost-Effectiveness at Reducing Crime Varies with Simultaneous Random Variation in Input Values

	Decrease in Number of Serious Crimes Per Additional Million Dollars			Difference in Number of Crimes Eliminated	
	Mandatory Minimums	Conventional Enforcement	Treating Heavy Users	Conv. Enf. vs. Man. Min.	Treatment vs. Man. Min.
Average	25.0	48.8	283.2	23.8	258.2
Variance	1059.8	4688.5	987.0	1520.6	198.0
Min, max, and percentiles					
Min	−75.3	−179.9	207.3	−144.2	136.7
1%	−32.1	−69.2	230.6	−42.0	212.4
5%	−17.9	−41.5	243.5	−23.1	235.3
25%	3.5	3.7	263.4	−0.1	253.7
50%	20.1	39.0	278.2	16.5	259.4
75%	41.1	81.7	296.5	39.3	263.3
95%	83.4	171.5	339.6	94.7	278.2
99%	131.8	268.2	390.7	157.2	296.9
Max	339.2	724.3	659.5	550.3	412.5

NOTE: Negative numbers indicate increases in crime.

prices it increased cocaine spending and, thus, cocaine-related crime. In those cases, mandatory minimums did not reduce cocaine-related crime; it merely failed to drive crime up as fast as did conventional enforcement. In only 715 of the trials (4.4 percent) did mandatory minimum sentencing both reduce crime and reduce crime by more than did conventional enforcement.

FEDERAL MANDATORY MINIMUM SENTENCING LAWS FOR DRUG OFFENSES

The following are verbatim texts of those provisions of the U.S. Code that establish mandatory minimum sentences for drug offenses.

21 U.S.C. §841—PROHIBITED ACTS

Unlawful Acts

(a) Except as authorized by this subchapter, it shall be unlawful for any person knowingly or intentionally—

    (1) to manufacture, distribute, or dispense, or possess with intent to manufacture, distribute, or dispense, a controlled substance; or

    (2) to create, distribute, or dispense, or possess with intent to distribute or dispense, a counterfeit substance.

Penalties

(b) Except as otherwise provided in section 859, 860, or 861 of this title, any person who violates subsection (a) of this section shall be sentenced as follows:

    (1) (A) In the case of a violation of subsection (a) of this section involving—

        (i) 1 kilogram or more of a mixture or substance containing a detectable amount of heroin;

(ii)   5 kilograms or more of a mixture or substance containing a detectable amount of—

    (I)   coca leaves, except coca leaves and extracts of coca leaves from which cocaine, ecgonine, and derivatives of ecgonine or their salts have been removed;

    (II)   cocaine, its salts, optical and geometric isomers, and salts of isomers;

    (III)   ecgonine, its derivatives, their salts, isomers, and salts of isomers; or

    (IV)   any compound, mixture, or preparation which contains any quantity of any of the substances referred to in subclauses (I) through (III);

(iii)   50 grams or more of a mixture or substance described in clause (ii) which contains cocaine base;

(iv)   100 grams or more of phencyclidine (PCP) or 1 kilogram or more of a mixture or substance containing a detectable amount of phencyclidine (PCP);

(v)   10 grams or more of a mixture or substance containing a detectable amount of lysergic acid diethylamide (LSD);

(vi)   400 grams or more of a mixture or substance containing a detectable amount of N-phenyl-N-[1-(2-phenylethyl)-4-piperidinyl] propanamide or 100 grams or more of a mixture or substance containing a detectable amount of any analogue of N-phenyl-N-[1-(2-phenylethyl)-4-piperidinyl] propanamide;

(vii)   1000 kilograms or more of a mixture or substance containing a detectable amount of marijuana, or 1,000 or more marijuana plants regardless of weight; or

(viii)   100 grams or more of methamphetamine, its salts, isomers, and salts of its isomers or 1 kilogram or more of a mixture or substance containing a detectable amount of methamphetamine, its salts, isomers, or salts of its isomers;

such person shall be sentenced to a term of imprisonment which may not be less than 10 years or more than life and if death or serious bodily injury results from the use of such substance shall be not less than 20 years or more than life, a fine not to exceed the greater of that authorized in accordance with the provisions of Title 18 or $4,000,000 if the defendant is an individual or $10,000,000 if the defendant is other than an individual, or both. If any person commits such a violation after a prior conviction for a felony drug offense has become final, such person shall be sentenced to a term of imprisonment which may not be less than 20 years and not more than life imprisonment and if death or serious bodily injury results from the use of such substance shall be sentenced to life imprisonment, a fine not to exceed the greater of twice that authorized in accordance with the provisions of Title 18, or $8,000,000 if the defendant is an individual or $20,000,000 if the defendant is other than an individual, or both. If any person commits a violation of this subparagraph or of section 849, 859, 860, or 861 of this title after two or more prior convictions for a felony drug offense have become final, such person shall be sentenced to a mandatory term of life imprisonment without release and fined in accordance with the preceding sentence. Any sentence under this subparagraph shall, in the absence of such a prior conviction, impose a term of supervised release of at least 5 years in addition to such term of imprisonment and shall, if there was such a prior conviction, impose a term of supervised release of at least 10 years in addition to such term of imprisonment. Notwithstanding any other provision of law, the court shall not place on probation or suspend the sentence of any person sentenced under this subparagraph. No person sentenced under this subparagraph shall be eligible for parole during the term of imprisonment imposed therein.

(B) In the case of a violation of subsection (a) of this section involving—

(i)   100 grams or more of a mixture or substance containing a detectable amount of heroin;

(ii)   500 grams or more of a mixture or substance containing a detectable amount of—

    (I)   coca leaves, except coca leaves and extracts of coca leaves from which cocaine, ecgonine, and derivatives of ecgonine or their salts have been removed;

    (II)   cocaine, its salts, optical and geometric isomers, and salts of isomers;

    (III)   ecgonine, its derivatives, their salts, isomers, and salts of isomers; or

    (IV)   any compound, mixture, or preparation which contains any quantity of any of the substances referred to in subclauses (I) through (III);

(iii)   5 grams or more of a mixture or substance described in clause (ii) which contains cocaine base;

(iv)   10 grams or more of phencyclidine (PCP) or 100 grams or more of a mixture or substance containing a detectable amount of phencyclidine (PCP);

(v)   1 gram or more of a mixture or substance containing a detectable amount of lysergic acid diethylamide (LSD);

(vi)   40 grams or more of a mixture or substance containing a detectable amount of N-phenyl-N-[1-(2-phenylethyl)-4-piperidinyl] propanamide or 10 grams or more of a mixture or substance containing a detectable amount of any analogue of N-phenyl-N-[1-(2-phenylethyl)-4-piperidinyl] propanamide;

(vii)   100 kilograms or more of a mixture or substance containing a detectable amount of marijuana, or 100 or more marijuana plants regardless of weight; or

(viii)   10 grams or more of methamphetamine, its salts, isomers, and salts of its isomers or 100 grams or more of a mixture or substance containing a detectable amount of methamphetamine, its salts, isomers, or salts of its isomers;

such person shall be sentenced to a term of imprisonment which may not be less than 5 years and not more than 40 years and if death or serious bodily injury results from the use of such substance shall be not less than 20 years or more than life, a fine not to exceed the greater of that authorized in accordance with the provisions of Title 18, or $2,000,000 if the defendant is an individual or $5,000,000 if the defendant is other than an individual, or both. If any person commits such a violation after a prior conviction for a felony drug offense has become final, such person shall be sentenced to a term of imprisonment which may not be less than 10 years and not more than life imprisonment and if death or serious bodily injury results from the use of such substance shall be sentenced to life imprisonment, a fine not to exceed the greater of twice that authorized in accordance with the provisions of Title 18, or $4,000,000 if the defendant is an individual or $10,000,000 if the defendant is other than an individual, or both. Any sentence imposed under this subparagraph shall, in the absence of such a prior conviction, include a term of supervised release of at least 4 years in addition to such term of imprisonment and shall, if there was such a prior conviction, include a term of supervised release of at least 8 years in addition to such term of imprisonment. Notwithstanding any other provision of law, the court shall not place on probation or suspend the sentence of any person sentenced under this subparagraph. No person sentenced under this subparagraph shall be eligible for parole during the term of imprisonment imposed therein.

21 U.S.C. §844—PENALTY FOR SIMPLE POSSESSION

(a) Unlawful acts; penalties

It shall be unlawful for any person knowingly or intentionally to possess a controlled substance unless such substance was obtained directly, or pursuant to a valid prescription or order, from a practitioner, while acting in the course of his professional practice, or except as otherwise authorized by this subchapter or subchapter II of this chapter. Any person who violates this subsection may be sentenced to a term of imprisonment of not more than 1 year, and shall be fined a minimum of $1,000, or both, except that if he commits such offense after a prior conviction under this subchapter or subchapter II of this chapter, or a prior conviction for any drug or narcotic offense chargeable under the law of any State, has become final, he shall be sentenced to a term of imprisonment for not less than 15 days but not more than 2 years, and shall be fined a minimum of $2,500, except, further, that if he commits such offense after two or more prior convictions under this subchapter or subchapter II of this chapter, or two or more prior convictions for any drug or narcotic offense chargeable under the law of any State, or a combination of two or more such offenses have become final, he shall be sentenced to a term of imprisonment for not less than 90 days but not more than 3 years, and shall be fined a minimum of $5,000. Notwithstanding the preceding sentence, a person convicted under this subsection for the possession of a mixture or substance which contains cocaine base shall be imprisoned not less than 5 years and not more than 20 years, and fined a minimum of $1,000, if the conviction is a first conviction under this subsection and the amount of the mixture or substance exceeds 5 grams, if the conviction is after a prior conviction for the possession of such a mixture or substance under this subsection becomes final and the amount of the mixture or substance exceeds 3 grams, or if the conviction is after 2 or more prior convictions for the possession of such a mixture or substance under this subsection become final and the amount of the mixture or substance exceeds 1 gram. The imposition or execution of a minimum sentence required to be imposed under this subsection shall not be suspended or deferred. Further, upon conviction, a person who violates this subsection shall be fined the reasonable costs of the investigation and prosecution of the offense, including the costs of prosecution of an offense as defined in sections 1918 and 1920 of Title 28, except that this sentence shall not apply and a fine under this section need not be imposed if the court determines under the provision of Title 18 that the defendant lacks the ability to pay.

(b) Repealed. Pub.L. 98–473, Title II, § 219(a), Oct. 12, 1984, 98 Stat. 2027

(c) "Drug or narcotic offense" defined

As used in this section, the term "drug or narcotic offense" means any offense which proscribes the possession, distribution, manufacture, cultivation, sale, transfer, or the attempt or conspiracy to possess, distribute, manufacture, cultivate, sell or transfer any substance the possession of which is prohibited under this subchapter.

[There are further provisions not reproduced here.]

21 U.S.C. §960—PROHIBITED IMPORT AND EXPORT

(a) Unlawful acts

Any person who—

    (1) contrary to section 952, 953, or 957 of this title, knowingly or intentionally imports or exports a controlled substance,

    (2) contrary to section 955 of this title, knowingly or intentionally brings or possesses on board a vessel, aircraft, or vehicle a controlled substance, or

    (3) contrary to section 959 of this title, manufactures, possesses with intent to distribute, or distributes a controlled substance,

shall be punished as provided in subsection (b) of this section.

(b) Penalties

    (1) In the case of a violation of subsection (a) of this section involving—

        (A) 1 kilogram or more of a mixture or substance containing a detectable amount of heroin;

        (B) 5 kilograms or more of a mixture or substance containing a detectable amount of—

            (i) coca leaves, except coca leaves and extracts of coca leaves from which cocaine, ecgonine, and derivatives of ecgonine or their salts have been removed;

(ii)   cocaine, its salts, optical and geometric isomers, and salts or[1] isomers;

(iii)   ecgonine, its derivatives, their salts, isomers, and salts of isomers; or

(iv)   any compound, mixture, or preparation which contains any quantity of any of the substances referred to in clauses (i) through (iii);

(C)   50 grams or more of a mixture or substance described in subparagraph (B) which contains cocaine base;

(D)   100 grams or more of phencyclidine (PCP) or 1 kilogram or more of a mixture or substance containing a detectable amount of phencyclidine (PCP);

(E)   10 grams or more of a mixture or substance containing a detectable amount of lysergic acid diethylamide (LSD);

(F)   400 grams or more of a mixture or substance containing a detectable amount of N-phenyl-N-[1-(2-phenylethyl)-4-piperidinyl] propanamide or 100 grams or more of a mixture or substance containing a detectable amount of any analogue of N-phenyl-N-[1-(2-phenylethyl)-4-piperidinyl] propanamide;

(G)   1000 kilograms or more of a mixture or substance containing a detectable amount of marihuana; or

(H)   100 grams or more of methamphetamine, its salts, isomers, and salts of its isomers or 1 kilogram or more of a mixture or substance containing a detectable amount of methamphetamine, its salts, isomers, or salts of its isomers.

the person committing such violation shall be sentenced to a term of imprisonment of not less than 10 years and not

---

[1] The original should likely be "of," not "or."

more than life and if death or serious bodily injury results from the use of such substance shall be sentenced to a term of imprisonment of not less than 20 years and not more than life, a fine not to exceed the greater of that authorized in accordance with the provisions of Title 18, or $4,000,000 if the defendant is an individual or $10,000,000 if the defendant is other than an individual, or both. If any person commits such a violation after a prior conviction for a felony drug offense has become final, such person shall be sentenced to a term of imprisonment of not less than 20 years and not more than life imprisonment and if death or serious bodily injury results from the use of such substance shall be sentenced to life imprisonment, a fine not to exceed the greater of twice that authorized in accordance with the provisions of Title 18, or $8,000,000 if the defendant is an individual or $20,000,000 if the defendant is other than an individual, or both. Any sentence under this paragraph shall, in the absence of such a prior conviction, impose a term of supervised release of at least 5 years in addition to such term of imprisonment and shall, if there was such a prior conviction, impose a term of supervised release of at least 10 years in addition to such term of imprisonment. Notwithstanding any other provision of law, the court shall not place on probation or suspend the sentence of any person sentenced under this paragraph. No person sentenced under this paragraph shall be eligible for parole during the term of imprisonment imposed therein.

(2)   In the case of a violation of subsection (a) of this section involving—

    (A)   100 grams or more of a mixture or substance containing a detectable amount of heroin;

    (B)   500 grams or more of a mixture or substance containing a detectable amount of—

        (i)   coca leaves, except coca leaves and extracts of coca leaves from which cocaine, ecgonine, and derivatives of ecgonine or their salts have been removed;

(ii)   cocaine, its salts, optical and geometric isomers, and salts or² isomers;

(iii)   ecgonine, its derivatives, their salts, isomers,
and salts of isomers; or

(iv)   any compound, mixture, or preparation which
contains any quantity of any of the substances
referred to in clauses (i) through (iii);

(C) 5 grams or more of a mixture or substance described
in subparagraph (B) which contains cocaine base;

(D) 10 grams or more of phencyclidine (PCP) or 100
grams or more of a mixture or substance containing a
detectable amount of phencyclidine (PCP);

(E) 1 gram or more of a mixture or substance containing
a detectable amount of lysergic acid diethylamide
(LSD);

(F) 40 grams or more of a mixture or substance containing a detectable amount of N-phenyl-N-[1-(2-
phenylethyl)-4-piperidinyl] propanamide or 10 grams
or more of a mixture or substance containing a
detectable amount of any analogue of N-phenyl-N-
[1-(2-phenylethyl)-4-piperidinyl] propanamide;

(G) 100 kilograms or more of a mixture or substance
containing a detectable amount of marihuana; or

(H) 10 grams or more of methamphetamine, its salts,
isomers, and salts of its isomers or 100 grams or more
of a mixture or substance containing a detectable
amount of methamphetamine, its salts, isomers, or
salts of its isomers.

the person committing such violation shall be sentenced to a
term of imprisonment of not less than 5 years and not more
than 40 years and if death or serious bodily injury results
from the use of such substance shall be sentenced to a term
of imprisonment of not less than twenty years and

---

²The original should likely be "of," not "or."

not more than life, a fine not to exceed the greater of that authorized in accordance with the provisions of Title 18, or $2,000,000 if the defendant is an individual or $5,000,000 if the defendant is other than an individual, or both. If any person commits such a violation after a prior conviction for a felony drug offense has become final, such person shall be sentenced to a term of imprisonment of not less than 10 years and not more than life imprisonment and if death or serious bodily injury results from the use of such substance shall be sentenced to life imprisonment, a fine not to exceed the greater of twice that authorized in accordance with the provisions of Title 18, or $4,000,000 if the defendant is an individual or $10,000,000 if the defendant is other than an individual, or both. Any sentence imposed under this paragraph shall, in the absence of such a prior conviction, include a term of supervised release of at least 4 years in addition to such term of imprisonment and shall, if there was such a prior conviction, include a term of supervised release of at least 8 years in addition to such term of imprisonment. Notwithstanding any other provision of law, the court shall not place on probation or suspend the sentence of any person sentenced under this paragraph. No person sentenced under this paragraph shall be eligible for parole during the term of imprisonment imposed therein.

(3) In the case of a violation under subsection (a) of this section involving a controlled substance in schedule I or II, the person committing such violation shall, except as provided in paragraphs (1), (2), and (4), be sentenced to a term of imprisonment of not more than 20 years and if death or serious bodily injury results from the use of such substance shall be sentenced to a term of imprisonment of not less than twenty years and not more than life, a fine not to exceed the greater of that authorized in accordance with the provisions of Title 18, or $1,000,000 if the defendant is an individual or $5,000,000 if the defendant is other than an individual, or both. If any person commits such a violation after a prior conviction for a felony drug offense has become final, such person shall be sentenced to a term of imprisonment of not more than 30 years and if death or serious bodily injury results from the use of such substance shall be sentenced to

life imprisonment, a fine not to exceed the greater of twice that authorized in accordance with the provisions of Title 18, or $2,000,000 if the defendant is an individual or $10,000,000 if the defendant is other than an individual, or both. Any sentence imposing a term of imprisonment under this paragraph shall, in the absence of such a prior conviction, impose a term of supervised release of at least 3 years in addition to such term of imprisonment and shall, if there was such a prior conviction, impose a term of supervised release of at least 6 years in addition to such term of imprisonment. Notwithstanding the prior sentence, and notwithstanding any other provision of law, the court shall not place on probation or suspend the sentence of any person sentenced under the provisions of this paragraph which provide for a mandatory term of imprisonment if death or serious bodily injury results, nor shall a person so sentenced be eligible for parole during the term of such a sentence.

(4) In the case of a violation under subsection (a) of this section with respect to less than 50 kilograms of marihuana, except in the case of 100 or more marihuana plants regardless of weight, less than 10 kilograms of hashish, less than one kilogram of hashish oil, or any quantity of a controlled substance in schedule III, IV, or V, the person committing such violation shall be imprisoned not more than five years, or be fined not to exceed the greater of that authorized in accordance with the provisions of Title 18, or $250,000 if the defendant is an individual or $1,000,000 if the defendant is other than an individual, or both. If a sentence under this paragraph provides for imprisonment, the sentence shall, in addition to such term of imprisonment, include (A) a term of supervised release of not less than two years if such controlled substance is in schedule I, II, III, or (B) a term of supervised release of not less than one year if such controlled substance is in schedule IV.

(c) Repealed. Pub.L. 98–473, Title II, § 225, Oct. 12, 1984, 98 Stat. 2030

(d) Penalty for importation or exportation. A person who knowingly or intentionally—

(1) imports or exports a listed chemical with intent to manufacture a controlled substance in violation of this subchapter or subchapter I of this chapter;

(2) exports a listed chemical in violation of the laws of the country to which the chemical is exported or serves as a broker or trader for an international transaction involving a listed chemical, if the transaction is in violation of the laws of the country to which the chemical is exported;

(3) imports or exports a listed chemical knowing, or having reasonable cause to believe, that the chemical will be used to manufacture a controlled substance in violation of this subchapter or subchapter I of this chapter;

(4) exports a listed chemical, or serves as a broker or trader for an international transaction involving a listed chemical, knowing, or having reasonable cause to believe, that the chemical will be used to manufacture a controlled substance in violation of the laws of the country to which the chemical is exported;

(5) imports or exports a listed chemical, with the intent to evade the reporting or recordkeeping requirements of section 971 of this title applicable to such importation or exportation by falsely representing to the Attorney General that the importation or exportation qualifies for a waiver of the 15-day notification requirement granted pursuant to section 971(e)(2) or (3) of this title by misrepresenting the actual country of final destination of the listed chemical or the actual listed chemical being imported or exported; or

(6) imports or exports a listed chemical in violation of section 957 or 971 of this title,

shall be fined in accordance with Title 18, imprisoned not more than 10 years, or both.

DERIVATION OF PARAMETER VALUES

PROBABILITY OF PROSECUTION GIVEN ARREST

According to the *Sourcebook of Criminal Justice Statistics—1994* (Maguire and Pastore, 1995, pp. 486–490), of 33,265 suspects in drug offense cases on which action was concluded by U.S. Attorneys in 1990, 25,094 (75.4 percent) were prosecuted, 1,758 (5.3 percent) were referred to U.S. magistrates (typically for prosecution as a misdemeanor), and the U.S. Attorneys declined to prosecute the remaining 6,413 (19.3 percent).[1]

The Bureau of Justice Statistics (1992a, p. 167) notes that 42 percent of cases declined for prosecution by U.S. Attorneys "were referred or handled in another prosecution including State court cases." Hence, many of those declined for prosecution may have faced conviction and sentencing not unlike those prosecuted as drug cases by the U.S. Attorneys. Thus we estimate an "effective probability of prosecution" as $0.754 + 0.42 \times 0.193 = 0.835$.

PROBABILITY OF TRIAL AND CONVICTION GIVEN CHARGE

The *Sourcebook* (Maguire and Pastore, 1994, Table 5.33, pp. 510–511) breaks down what happened to defendants charged with drug law violations in U.S. District Courts in 1990. (See Table B.1.) Of a total

---

[1]For simplicity, we assume here and elsewhere that drug offenses give rise to drug-related charges. In fact, this is not always the case. Individuals arrested for an apparent drug offense may be prosecuted for a different crime.

Table B.1

Prosecution of Federal Drug Offenders in 1990

	Not Convicted		Convicted		Total	
Dismissed	2,610	(13.54%)	0		2,610	(13.54%)
Court trial (i.e., no jury)	53	(0.28%)	148	(0.77%)	201	(1.04%)
Jury trial	420	(2.18%)	2,973	(15.43%)	3,393	(17.61%)
Guilty or nolo con- tendere plea	0		13,067	(67.81%)	13,067	(67.81%)
Total	3,083	(16.00%)	16,188	(84.00%)	19,271	(100%)

of 19,271 charged, 3,083 were not convicted (16.0 percent) and 16,188 were convicted (84.0 percent); 3,594 (18.6 percent) went to trial (court or jury), and 3,121 of those (86.8 percent) were convicted.

SENTENCE GIVEN CONVICTION

The *Sourcebook* (Maguire and Pastore, 1994, Table 5.33, pp. 510–511) gives information on sentences of those convicted of federal drug law violations in 1990. Of 16,188 convicted, 13,838 (85.48 percent) were imprisoned (including 59 life sentences). Terms served are given in Chapter Six. The average term for federal offenders was 2.26 years.

FINES GIVEN CONVICTION

The Bureau of Justice Statistics (1992b, p. 188) reports that 20 percent of sentenced federal drug offenders were required to pay fines and restitution in 1990. Table 12 of *Felony Sentences in State Courts* (Bureau of Justice Statistics, 1992c) says that 20 percent of persons convicted of drug trafficking were given a fine and 12 percent were required to pay restitution. It is not clear whether the 12 percent is a subset of the 20 percent, or in addition to them, and there is no data on the magnitude of restitution payments, so we will assume that 20 percent are assessed penalties of a magnitude equal to the average fine. This average for a drug offender convicted of something other than simple possession was $19,810, suggesting that the expected fine was $3,962. No data were given on the fraction of these fines that were paid. We assume with little basis that roughly half the fines are paid, so the expected fine paid per conviction is $2,000.

ESTIMATING THE VALUE OF DRUGS SEIZED

The DEA's STRIDE database records all drug samples that are analyzed in DEA laboratories. Most of these are samples acquired by the DEA, FBI, or the Washington, D.C. metropolitan police. Cocaine observations for 1990 and 1991 from these three sources were analyzed for this project.

By regressing log price on log quantity for purchase observations, it was determined that the value of cocaine in 1990 and 1991 was about $100 $X^{0.765}$, where X is the transaction size in raw (not pure) grams. See Caulkins (1994) for details on analysis of STRIDE cocaine price data. The method used here is simpler than that in Caulkins (1994), because above 5 grams the vast majority of cocaine observations have very high purities, so there is little need to adjust for variation in purity.

The formula above was used to estimate the value of all 6,883 STRIDE cocaine observations associated with the DEA or FBI in those years that were large enough to trigger a mandatory minimum sentence. Table B.2 shows their number and average value broken down by type of cocaine (crack versus powder) and length of sentence they triggered. The overall average value of drugs seized that could trigger a 5-year mandatory minimum sentence (but not a 10-year sentence) was $16,600 (i.e., it was the average of 2,951 powder seizures worth an average of $25,718 and 1,709 crack seizures worth an average of $944). For 10-year sentences the corresponding figure was $332,600. For all mandatory-minimum-triggering seizures (i.e., for all four elements in the data columns), the average value was $118,694.

More than one arrest may be associated with each seizure, however. The DEA made 21,799 drug arrests in 1990 (Bureau of Justice Statistics, 1992a, p. 158), and STRIDE records 4,619 cocaine seizure observations associated with the DEA. In 1993, 51.7 percent of the DEA's drug arrests were associated with cocaine (Maguire and

Table B.2

**Number and Average Value of 1990 and 1991 STRIDE
Observations Large Enough to Trigger
Mandatory Minimum Sentences**

	Powder Cocaine		Crack Cocaine	
5-year sentence	$25,718	5-year sentence	$944	
(500–5,000 grams)	(n = 2,951)	(5–50 grams)	(n = 1,709)	
10-year sentence	$625,888	10-year sentence	$16,649	
(5,000+ grams)	(n = 1,153)	(50+ grams)	(n = 1,070)	

Pastore, 1994, Table 4.42, p. 465). If the fraction of DEA arrests that were associated with cocaine was the same in 1990 as it was in 1993, that suggests that there are 21,799 × 0.517/4,619 = 2.44 arrests per DEA seizure. Hence, we assume that the average value of drugs seized per qualifying arrest is $118,694/2.44 = $48,646.

VALUE OF ASSETS SEIZED

The ONDCP (1992, p. 94) reports that the DEA seized $27,518 worth of assets per arrest in 1991 and an estimated $27,574 per arrest in 1992. For the FBI it reports (p. 99) seizures of $19,687 and $19,383 per investigation completed in 1991 and 1992, respectively. Likewise, Organized Crime Drug Enforcement Task Forces (OCDETF) are credited (p. 121) with $74,112 and $74,443 in seizures per individual indicted in 1991 and 1992, respectively.

Not all assets seized are ultimately forfeited. The Bureau of Justice Statistics (1992a, p. 156) reports that in 1990 the DEA seized "more than one billion" in assets and kept $427 million, suggesting that about $11,000 in assets are forfeited per DEA arrest. The ONDCP (1992, p. 121) reports that OCDETF forfeitures in 1991 and 1992 were 25.3 percent of seizures, suggesting that about $19,000 in assets are forfeited per individual indicted by the OCDETF. We assume that $15,000 in assets are forfeited per qualifying arrest, on average.

QUANTITY OF COCAINE CONSUMED AND AMOUNT SPENT

Both Everingham and Rydell (1994) and Rhodes et al. (1995) have estimated the size and value of the cocaine market. We use those of the former. The reason is that the two estimates are quite close and the efficacy of treatment estimates used here are taken from Rydell and Everingham (1994), who use the Everingham and Rydell cocaine market size estimates.[2] For completeness, we summarize the figures from both studies.

Rhodes et al. (1995) estimate the number of hard-core and occasional cocaine users in 1992 and their weekly spending on cocaine. Combining these numbers gives an estimate of total dollar spending on cocaine of $33.1 billion. (See Table B.3.)

They assume that payments in-kind for cocaine that were worth $3.4 billion, were made to drug sellers, so the total equivalent retail sales would be $36.5 billion. They think the retail price was between $130 and $163 per pure gram, so that total consumption was between 224 and 280 metric tons of cocaine. An average figure of $146.50 per pure gram implies that consumption was about 250 metric tons. Rhodes et al.'s (1995) dollar figures are given in 1994 dollars; they can be

Table B.3

Rhodes et al.'s Estimates of the Size of the Cocaine Market

	Hard-core Users	Occasional Users	Total
No. of users[a]	2,339,381	4,330,521	6,669,902
Weekly spending per user[b]	$231	$34	
Annual spending per user	$12,012	$1,768	
Total annual spending	$25.5 billion[c]	$7.656 billion	$33.1 billion

[a]Rhodes et al., 1995, p. 12.

[b]Rhodes et al., 1995, p. 14.

[c]$25.5 billion does not equal 2,339,381 × 52 × $231. No explanation was given by Rhodes et al. (1995) as to this apparent discrepancy.

---

[2]It is not immediately clear without replicating Rydell and Everingham's entire analysis, how, if at all, those treatment efficacy estimates should be adjusted if we were to make a different assumption about the size of the market.

roughly converted to 1992 dollars by dividing by 1.056, which is the ratio of the consumer price index for all urban consumers in December of 1993 to the same index in January of 1992.

Rydell and Everingham (1994) estimate that in 1992 there were 1.7 million heavy users (p. 17) consuming 120 grams per year (p. 24) and 5.6 million light users (p. 17) consuming one-eighth as much (p. 18) per capita as do heavy users, or about 15 grams per year. Multiplying the user numbers by the rates and adding the products gives 288 metric tons per year of consumption, which differs only by round-off error from the figure of 291 metric tons that they give (p. 58). At a retail price of $129.20 per pure gram (p. 59), that implies that consumers spent $37.6 billion on cocaine in 1992.

These estimates are summarized in Table B.4.

Table B.4

Estimates of the Size of the Cocaine Market

Study	Consumption (metric tons)	1992 Price ($/pure gram retail)	Spending (billions of 1992 $)
Rhodes et al. (1995)	250	$137–$172	$34.9
Rydell and Everingham (1994)	291	$129.20	$37.6

DERIVATION OF EQUATIONS IN TABLE 7.1

Chapter Seven estimated how spending more on various drug control programs would affect (1) the costs enforcement imposes on drug dealers and (2) demand. This appendix derives expressions for the changes in the quantity of drugs consumed, market price, and amount users pay for drugs associated with a 1 percent increase in enforcement and those associated with a 1 percent increase in demand by solving for the intersection of the supply and demand curves.

DEMAND CURVE

Recall that the demand curve is modeled as being locally linear around the current market equilibrium, with its slope determined by the elasticity of demand. If we let the subscript $_0$ denote quantities pertaining to the original market equilibrium, this can be written as:

$$Q_D(P) = Q_0\left(1 + \eta\left(\frac{P}{P_0} - 1\right)\right) ,$$

where

P	=	market clearing price,
$Q_D(P)$	=	quantity demanded at a market price of P,
P_0	=	market price in the initial equilibrium, and
Q_0	=	market clearing quantity in the initial equilibrium.

It is convenient to invert this expression, to express price as a function of the quantity demanded at that price:

$$P_D(Q) = P_0\left[1 + \frac{1}{\eta}\left(\frac{Q}{Q_0} - 1\right)\right] .$$

SUPPLY CURVE

Recall the assumptions that: (1) in equilibrium, dealers' revenues just cover their costs and (2) there are three types of costs: (a) normal business costs—the per unit cost of which increases linearly with quantity as in a standard linear supply curve, (b) costs that are proportional to the dollar value of the market, and (c) costs that are proportional to enforcement. Hence, we can write

$$P_s(Q)Q = (c + dQ)Q + E + \gamma(PQ) .$$

where

$P_s(Q)$	=	supply curve,
Q	=	market clearing quantity,
$c + dQ$	=	regular business costs per unit sold,
E	=	enforcement (denominated in dollars of costs imposed on suppliers), and
γ	=	fraction of supplier costs that are proportional to value of drugs sold.

Solving for P yields the supply curve:

$$P_s(Q) = K + LQ + \frac{E}{(1-\gamma)Q}$$

where for convenience we have introduced $K = c/(1 - \gamma)$ and $L = d/(1 - \gamma)$.

The goal is to derive expressions for changes in market quantity, price, and revenues as a function of parameters such as γ that describe what fraction of dealers' costs in the original market equilibrium are attributable to different causes. Hence, it is necessary to introduce parameters for the remaining fractions. Let β be the fraction of dealers' costs in the initial equilibrium that is attributable to enforcement. That is,

$$\beta = \frac{E_0}{P_0 Q_0} \quad .$$

Let α_0 and α_1 be defined similarly for the normal business costs. That is,

$$\alpha_0 = \frac{c Q_0}{P_0 Q_0} \quad \text{and}$$

$$\alpha_1 = \frac{d Q_0^2}{P_0 Q_0} \quad .$$

THE IMPACT OF INCREASING ENFORCEMENT

Suppose enforcement were increased by $100 r$ percent so that $E = (1 + r) E_0$. We can find the new market equilibrium quantity (Q) by solving for the intersection of the supply and demand curves, i.e., by setting $P_s(Q) = P_D(Q)$:

$$P_s(Q) = K + L Q + \frac{(1+r) E_0}{(1-\gamma) Q} = P_0 \left[1 + \frac{1}{\eta} \left(\frac{Q}{Q_0} - 1 \right) \right] = P_D(Q) \quad .$$

Introduce the notation $q = Q/Q_0$ and $\Delta q = (Q - Q_0)/Q_0$. Note that $Q = (1 + \Delta q) Q_0$. From the initial equilibrium, we know that

$$E_0 = (1 - \gamma) Q_0 (P_0 - K - L Q_0) \quad ,$$

so

$$K + LQ + \frac{(1+r)(1-\gamma)Q_0(P_0 - K - LQ_0)}{(1-\gamma)(1+\Delta q)Q_0} = P_0\left[1 + \frac{\Delta q}{\eta}\right]$$

and thus

$$\left(P_0 - K - LQ_0\right)\left(\Delta q - r\right) + \left(\frac{P_0}{\eta} - LQ_0\right)\Delta q\left(1 + \Delta q\right) = 0 \quad .$$

Note that

$$\frac{\left(P_0 - K - LQ_0\right)}{\dfrac{P_0}{\eta} - LQ_0} = \frac{\dfrac{E_0}{(1-\gamma)Q_0}}{\dfrac{P_0}{\eta} - \dfrac{dQ_0}{(1-\gamma)}} = \frac{\dfrac{E_0\eta}{P_0Q_0}}{1 - \gamma - \dfrac{\eta dQ_0^2}{P_0Q_0}} = \frac{\beta\eta}{1 - \gamma - \alpha_1\eta}$$

Call this quantity Y. Then the intersection of the supply and demand curves is defined by:

$$Y\left(\Delta q - r\right) + \Delta q\left(1 + \Delta q\right) = 0$$

so

$$\left(\Delta q\right)^2 + \left(1 + Y\right)\Delta q - rY = 0 \quad .$$

The quadratic formula implies

$$\Delta q = \frac{-(1+Y) \pm \sqrt{(1+Y)^2 + 4rY}}{2} \quad .$$

Since $\Delta q = 0$ when $r = 0$, we are interested in the positive root.

The derivative of Δq with respect to r, with r set equal to 0, gives the percentage change in the market clearing quantity associated with a 1 percent increase in enforcement effort.

$$\frac{d\Delta q}{dr} = \frac{1}{2}\frac{1}{2}\frac{4Y}{\sqrt{(1+Y)^2 + 4rY}} \cdot$$

With $r = 0$, this reduces to

$$\frac{d\Delta q}{dr} = \frac{Y}{1+Y} = \frac{\beta\eta}{1 - \gamma + (\beta - \alpha_1)\eta} \cdot$$

THE IMPACT OF INCREASING DEMAND

Suppose demand increased by $100s$ percent. This would change the original demand curve to

$$Q_D(P) = (1+s)Q_0\left(1 + \eta\left(\frac{P}{P_0} - 1\right)\right) ,$$

and the inverted demand curve to

$$P_D(Q) = P_0\left[1 + \frac{1}{\eta}\left(\frac{Q}{(1+s)Q_0}\right) - 1\right] .$$

The effect of such a change on the market clearing quantity (Q) can be found by solving for the intersection of the original supply curve (with $E = E_0$) and this new demand curve, i.e., by setting:

$$P_s(Q) = K + LQ + \frac{E_0}{(1-\gamma)Q} = P_0\left[1 + \frac{1}{\eta}\left(\frac{Q}{(1+s)Q_0} - 1\right)\right] = P_D(Q)$$

so

$$K + LQ + \frac{(1-\gamma)Q_0(P_0 - K - LQ_0)}{(1-\gamma)(1+\Delta q)Q_0} = P_0\left[1 + \frac{1}{\eta}\left(\frac{(1+\Delta q)Q_0}{(1+s)Q_0} - 1\right)\right] .$$

Let $x = 1 + \Delta q$. Then

$$\left(P_0 - K - LQ_0\right)\left(1 - \frac{1}{x}\right) + \frac{P_0}{\eta}\left(\frac{x}{1+s} - 1\right) - LQ_0(x - 1) = 0.$$

For convenience, let

$A = P_0 - K - LQ_0,$

$B = P_0 / \eta$, and

$C = LQ_0.$

Then

$$A(x - 1) + \left(\frac{B}{1+s} - C\right)x^2 + (C - B)x = 0$$

so

$$x = \frac{(B - C) - A \pm \sqrt{\left(A - (B - C)\right)^2 + 4A\left(\frac{B}{1+s} - C\right)}}{2\left(\frac{B}{1+s} - C\right)}.$$

When $s = 0$, $x = 1$, so we are interested in the positive root. Since x differs from Δq by a constant, their derivatives are the same. Thus, when $s = 0$,

$$\frac{d\Delta q}{ds} = \frac{(B - C) - A + \sqrt{\left(A + (B - C)\right)^2}}{2}\left(\frac{B}{(B - C)^2}\right) +$$

$$\frac{1}{2(B-C)}\frac{1}{2}\frac{(-4AB)}{\sqrt{(A+(B-C))^2}}$$

$$=\frac{B}{A+(B-C)}$$

$$=\frac{\dfrac{P_0}{\eta}}{P_0-K-LQ+\dfrac{P_0}{\eta}-LQ_0}$$

$$=\frac{\dfrac{1}{\eta}}{\dfrac{\beta}{1-\gamma}+\dfrac{1}{\eta}-\dfrac{\alpha_1}{1-\gamma}}=\frac{1-\gamma}{1-\gamma+(\beta-\alpha_1)\eta}\quad.$$

RELATIONSHIP BETWEEN CHANGES IN PRICE, CONSUMPTION, AND DOLLAR VALUE OF THE MARKET

Above we derived expressions for the percentage change in consumption associated with a 1 percent increase in either enforcement or demand. Now we want similar expressions for the changes in price and the dollar value of the market.

When enforcement increases, the supply curve shifts, and the equilibrium moves along the fixed demand curve. The price elasticity of demand is η, so

$$\frac{d\Delta p}{dr}=\frac{1}{\eta}\frac{d\Delta q}{dr}=\frac{\beta}{1-\gamma+(\beta-\alpha_1)\eta}\quad.$$

When r is zero, $p=q=1$, so the rate of change in the amount spent is simply the sum of the rates of change in the price and quantity consumed, i.e.,

$$\frac{d\Delta pq}{dr} = \frac{d\Delta p}{dr}q + p\frac{d\Delta q}{dr} = \frac{\beta(1+\eta)}{1-\gamma+(\beta-\alpha_1)\eta} \quad .$$

When demand changes, the equilibrium moves along the fixed supply curve. In that case,

$$\Delta p = \frac{P - P_0}{P_0} = \frac{K + LQ + \frac{E_0}{(1-\gamma)Q} - \left(K + LQ_0 + \frac{E_0}{(1-\gamma)Q_0}\right)}{P_0}$$

$$= \frac{d(Q - Q_0)}{(1-\gamma)P_0} + \frac{E_0}{(1-\gamma)P_0}\left(\frac{1}{Q} - \frac{1}{Q_0}\right)$$

$$= \frac{\alpha_1}{(1-\gamma)}\Delta q - \frac{\beta}{(1-\gamma)}\frac{Q_0}{Q}\Delta q \quad .$$

Since, when $s = 0$, $Q = Q_0$,

$$\Delta p = \frac{(\alpha_1 - \beta)}{(1-\gamma)}\Delta q,$$

and thus, when $s = 0$,

$$\frac{d\Delta p}{ds} = \frac{(\alpha_1 - \beta)}{1-\gamma+(\beta-\alpha_1)\eta} \quad .$$

By an argument parallel to that above, the change in the amount spent on drugs is

$$\frac{d\Delta pq}{ds} = \frac{1-\gamma-(\beta-\alpha_1)}{1-\gamma+(\beta-\alpha_1)\eta} \quad .$$

Table 7.1, reproduced here as Table C.1, summarizes these results.

Table C.1

How Market Quantities Respond When Enforcement or Demand Changes

Percentage Change in	If There Is a	
	1% Increase in Costs that Enforcement Imposes on Dealers	1% Increase in Demand
Consumption =	$\dfrac{\beta\eta}{1-\gamma+(\beta-\alpha_1)\eta}$	$\dfrac{1-\gamma}{1-\gamma+(\beta-\alpha_1)\eta}$
Price =	$\dfrac{\beta}{1-\gamma+(\beta-\alpha_1)\eta}$	$\dfrac{\alpha_1-\beta}{1-\gamma+(\beta-\alpha_1)\eta}$
Spending =	$\dfrac{\beta(1+\eta)}{1-\gamma+(\beta-\alpha_1)\eta}$	$\dfrac{1-\gamma-(\beta-\alpha_1)}{1-\gamma+(\beta-\alpha_1)\eta}$

Note: the expressions in the table are valid only if the original equilibrium was stable. A necessary and sufficient condition for the stability of the initial equilibrium is that when $Q = Q_0$

$$\frac{dP_s(Q)}{dQ} > \frac{dP_D(Q)}{dQ}$$

which reduces to the condition $1 - \gamma + (\beta - \alpha_1)\eta > 0$.

ESTIMATING THE RELATIONSHIP BETWEEN DRUG MARKETS AND CRIME

This appendix describes how the "conversion factors" for converting from changes in cocaine consumption and spending to changes in crime were derived. The overall strategy is simple. We estimate the current amount of drug-related crime and what fraction of that is related to cocaine. We divide by the current levels of consumption or spending to find the average amount of crime per unit of spending or consumption and then assume the marginal rate equals the average rate.

The task is divided into three pieces, according to Goldstein's (1985) tripartite framework for categorizing drug-related crime into (a) economic-compulsive, (b) psychopharmacological, and (c) systemic crime. Economic-compulsive and systemic crime are assumed to be proportional to drug spending because they are market-related forms of crime. Psychopharmacological crime, in contrast, is a function of drug use and, hence, is assumed to be proportional to the quantity of a drug consumed.

AMOUNT OF DRUG-RELATED CRIME

Economic-Compulsive Crime

The 1993 *Sourcebook* (Maguire and Pastore, 1994[1]) gives fractions of various offenses that prison inmates report were committed to get money for drugs. Similar data are available for jail inmates from 1989

---

[1]Quoting the U.S. Department of Justice, Bureau of Justice Statistics, *Correctional Populations in the United States, 1991*, NCJ-142729, USGPO, Washington, D.C., p. 35.

(see Bureau of Justice Statistics, 1994, p. 8). These are reported in Table D.1.

Assuming that proportions for all offenders are similar to those for currently incarcerated offenders, these proportions can be multiplied by total crime figures to estimate the number of economic-compulsive drug-related crimes (see Table D.2). Note: these are

Table D.1

Proportions of Crime Committed to Get Money to Buy Drugs
(in percentage)

Crime	Prison Inmates	Jail Inmates	Our Estimate of a Consensus Figure
Homicide	5.3	3	4
Sexual assault	4.4	2	0
Robbery	26.8	32	30
Assault	5.5	3	5
Aggravated assault	6		5
Simple assault	6		5
Burglary	29.6	31	30
Larceny	31.0	27.8	30
Auto theft	16.4	6.8	7

NOTE: We take sexual assault to be 0 percent because it is unclear how sexual assault would either generate income or follow directly from a crime committed to gain income (in the way some robberies turn into homicides).

Table D.2

Number of Economic-Compulsive Drug-Related Crimes

Crime	U.S. Total	Proportion Economic-Compulsive	Number Economic-Compulsive
Homicide	23,800	4%	950
Sexual assault	141,000	0%	0
Robbery	1,230,000	30%	368,000
Agg. assault	1,850,000	5%	92,400
Simple assault	3,410,000	5%	170,000
Burglary	4,760,000	30%	1,430,000
Larceny	20,300,000	30%	6,090,000
Auto theft	1,960,000	7%	137,000

conservative estimates because drug use can reduce licit earnings potential (e.g., when someone loses a job because they fail a drug test), which might induce people to commit crime to finance purchases of things other than drugs.

Psychopharmacological Violence

According to the Drug-Related Crime Analysis–Homicide 1 (DRCA-H1), as reported by Goldstein, Brownstein, and Ryan (1992), 25 percent of the 309 homicides committed in New York State outside of New York City in 1984 were primarily psychopharmacological. An additional 6 percent were classified as multidimensional, and some of those may have had a psychopharmacological component. The vast majority of the 30 percent total was related to alcohol.

They also report in their DRCA-H2 study that 14 percent of 218 drug-related New York City homicides studied had a psychopharmacological component. About 27.5 percent of those were primarily related to illicit drugs.

Spunt et al. (1995) report that in their study of drug relationships in murder (DREIM), 16 percent of respondents reported that the homicide they committed was related to their being high on an illicit drug, and half of those (8 percent) said the drug in question was cocaine.

Spunt et al. (1990) described studies of drug-related involvement in violent episodes by males (DRIVE) and females (FEMDRIVE). About 15 percent of violent events committed by a sample of street drug users had a psychopharmacological dimension related only to illicit drug use. Another 15–20 percent were alcohol-related (so that a total of about 33 percent had some psychopharmacological dimension).

Drugs and Crime Facts, 1993 (Bureau of Justice Statistics, 1994) reports that the percentage of victimizations where the victim perceived the offender to be under the influence was as indicated in Table D.3. In each case, 40–60 percent of the time the victim did not know whether the person was under the influence, so the actual fractions in which the assailant was under the influence might be twice as great as those reported in the table.

Table D.3

Percentage of Victims Perceiving Offender as Intoxicated

Crime	Drugs Only	Drugs and Alcohol	Combined
Rape	4.2	5.5	9.7
Robbery	3.8	3.1	6.9
Agg. assault	4.3	8.1	12.4
Simple assault	2.4	4.8	7.2

Considering all of these disparate pieces of evidence, it seems that on the order of 12 percent of violent crime is psychopharmacological in nature and related to illicit drugs, although the fraction for homicide may be lower than for other types of crime. Our assumptions of these fractions and their implications for the number of drug-related psychopharmacological crimes are listed in Table D.4.

Systemic Violence

Goldstein, Brownstein, and Ryan (1992) show that the fraction of homicides that are systemic may be between 10 and 40. For all violent events committed by street drug users, the fraction may be 26 percent for men (DRIVE) and 13 percent for women (FEMDRIVE) (Goldstein et al. 1991).

The study by Reuter, MacCoun, and Murphy, (1990, p. 104) says street dealers in Washington, D.C., have a 1.4 percent death risk, and in 1987 there were 14,000 "regular" (full-time-equivalent) cocaine dealers in Washington, D.C. Since Washington's metropolitan area

Table D.4

Number of Psychopharmacological Crimes

Crime	U.S. Total	Proportion Psycho- pharmacological	Number Psycho- pharmacological
Homicide	23,800	7.5%	1,780
Sexual assault	141,000	10%	14,100
Agg. assault	1,850,000	15%	277,000
Simple assault	3,410,000	12%	409,000

had 482 homicides in 1991, that suggests that 40 percent of those homicides were related to cocaine selling.

The Bureau of Justice Statistics' (1993, p. 8) estimates of drug-related homicides give a much lower estimate (decreasing from 7.4 percent to 5.7 percent between 1989 and 1992).

Bureau of Justice Statistics (1993) also describes a study of murder cases[2] disposed in the nation's 75 most populous counties and found that circumstances involving illegal drugs, such as a drug scam or dispute over drugs, accounted for 18 percent of defendants and 16 percent of victims. Note, the portion of drug-market-related homicides leading to filing of charges is probably lower than the analogous portion for other homicides, e.g., between family members. Thus, these numbers probably somewhat understate the proportion of all homicides that are drug market related.

Combining these pieces of information, one might guess that on the order of one-fifth of assaults, homicides, and aggravated assaults are systemic (Table D.5).

THE PROPORTION OF DRUG-RELATED CRIME THAT IS RELATED TO COCAINE

Economic-Compulsive Crime

Since economic-compulsive crime is related to drug spending, at first blush one might expect that cocaine's fraction of economic-

Table D.5

Proportion of Homicides and Assaults Systemic to the Drug Market

Crime	U.S. Total	Proportion Systemic	Number Systemic
Homicide	23,800	20%	4,750
Agg. assault	1,850,000	20%	370,000
Simple assault	3,410,000	20%	681,000

---

[2]*Murder in Large Urban Counties, 1988.* Federal Bureau of Investigation.

compulsive drug-related crime would be the same as cocaine's fraction of drug-related spending, about which we have information from Rhodes et al. (1995). However, a greater deal of marijuana spending is done by people who do not spend a very large fraction of their disposable income on drugs (which is not the case for cocaine or heroin), suggesting that economic-compulsive crime may be driven by spending on illicit drugs other than marijuana. Of course, some compulsive cocaine users who rob and steal to finance their cocaine habit also buy marijuana; for them, spending more on either drug would presumably generate an additional incentive to commit crime. Hence, we need to account for the quantity of marijuana consumed by these "hard-core" users of the expensive drugs (cocaine and heroin).

The Drug Use Forecasting System finds that roughly 15–40 percent of arrestees in urban areas test positive for marijuana (NIJ, 1993). There are roughly 2.5 million heavy drug users prone to commit economic-compulsive drug-related crime (ONDCP, 1995). Suppose, then, that of these, 25 percent consume marijuana, and that they do it at a rate double that reported by Rhodes et al. (1995, Table 6, p. 20) as average for respondents to the National Household Survey on Drug Abuse. Then consumption of marijuana by those heavy users would have been

Year	1988	1989	1990	1991	1992	1993
Spending	$1.0 B	$1.0 B	$1.2 B	$1.2 B	$1.4 B	$1.3 B

Combining these estimates with Rhodes et al.'s (1995, p. 5) estimates of spending on cocaine, heroin, marijuana, and other drugs, one can obtain a rough estimate of the fraction of economic-compulsive crimes over these years that were related to cocaine. This is done by dividing spending on cocaine by spending on all drugs except for marijuana not consumed by heavy users. The results (Table D.6) suggest that about 75 percent of economic-compulsive drug-related crime is related to cocaine.

Systemic and Psychopharmacological Crime

One approach to estimating the fraction of drug-related systemic crime that is related to cocaine parallels that just taken for economic-

Table D.6

Spending on Illicit Drugs
(in billions of dollars)

Spending on	1988	1989	1990	1991	1992	1993
Cocaine	$41.1	$42.5	$38.9	$35.2	$33.1	$30.8
Heroin	$11.2	$11.5	$10.3	$8.2	$7.0	$7.1
Marijuana	$8.9	$9.0	$9.6	$9.0	$10.1	$9.0
Other drugs	$3.2	$2.8	$2.3	$2.4	$2.2	$1.8
Total	$64.4	$65.8	$61.1	$54.8	$52.4	$48.7
Marijuana by heavy users	$1.0	$1.0	$1.2	$1.2	$1.4	$1.3
Cocaine's fraction of economic-compulsive crime	72.8%	73.5%	73.8%	75.0%	75.7%	75.2%

compulsive crime but excludes marijuana spending completely on the grounds that most marijuana dealers are not very violent. This would give fractions over time of

Year	1988	1989	1990	1991	1992	1993
Systemic	74.1%	74.8%	75.5%	76.9%	78.3%	77.6%

Another approach is to draw on the homicide studies of Goldstein and his colleagues (Table D.7). In the table we give each drug equal weight when multiple drugs were listed for a homicide. When the exact drugs were not identified (e.g., "other multiple"), those observations are excluded. The DREIM study information does not exactly fit into this taxonomy. The questions asked there were "Was homicide related to being high?" and "Was it related to some other drug status?" Many of the noncocaine reports for that study were for marijuana. If those were excluded on the assumption that little psychopharmacological or systemic drug-related crime is due to marijuana, the psychopharmacological share for cocaine would rise to 73 percent and the "other" share to 62 percent.

Overall it would appear that on the order of 50 percent of the illicit psychopharmacological and 75 percent of systemic drug-related homicides are related to cocaine. For lack of better data, these same fractions will be applied to all crimes, not just homicides.

Table D.7

Homicides' Relationship to Cocaine and Other Drugs

Data Set	Number of Homicides Related to		
	Cocaine	All Other Illicit	Cocaine's Fraction
DRCA-H1			
Psychopharm. crime	0	6	0%
Systemic crime	8.5	5	63%
DRCA-H2			
Economic-compulsive crime	8	0	100%
Psychopharm. crime	7	1.5	82.4%
Systemic crime	147.5	9.5	93.9%
DREIM			
Psychopharm. crime	22	30	42%
Other crime	13	15	46%

SOURCES: Goldstein et al. (1989); Goldstein, Brownstein, and Ryan (1992); and Spunt et al. (1995).

OVERALL RESULTS

Table D.8 summarizes the conversion factors we use in Chapter Four and the calculations underlying their derivation.

Table D.8

Estimated Relationship Among Drug Use, Consumption, and Crime

	Homicide	Sexual Assault	Aggrav. Assault	Simple Assault	Robbery	Burglary	Larceny	Auto Theft
No. of crimes/yr	23,760	140,930	1,848,530	3,406,160	1,225,510	4,757,420	20,311,980	1,958,780
Psychopharmacological								
% drug-related	*7.5*	*10*	*15*	*12*				
No. drug-related	1,782	14,093	277,280	408,739				
% cocaine-related	*50*	*50*	*50*	*50*				
No. cocaine-related	891	7,047	138,640	204,370				
Crimes/metric ton	3.06	24.21	476.43	702.30				
Econ-compulsive								
% drug-related	*4*		*5*	*5*	*30*	*30*	*30*	*7*
No. drug-related	950		92,427	170,308	367,653	1,427,226	6,093,594	137,115
% cocaine-related	*75*		*75*	*75*	*75*	*75*	*75*	*75*
No. cocaine-related	713		69,320	127,731	275,740	1,070,420	4,570,196	102,836
Crime/$ billion	19		1,844	3,397	7,334	28,471	121,557	2,735
Systemic								
% drug-related	*20*		*20*	*20*				
No. drug-related	4,752		369,706	681,232				
% cocaine-related	*75*		*75*	*75*				
No. cocaine-related	3,564		277,280	510,924				
Crime/$ billion	95		7,375	13,589				
Econ-compulsive + systemic crimes/$ billion	114		9,219	16,987	7,334	28,471	121,557	2,735

Boyum, David Anders. 1992. *Reflections on Economic Theory and Drug Enforcement*, Ph.D. Thesis in Public Policy, Harvard University, Cambridge, Mass.

Brownstein, Henry H., Hari R. Shiledar Baxi, Paul J. Goldstein, and Patrick J. Ryan. 1992. "The Relationship of Drugs, Drug Trafficking, and Drug Traffickers to Homicide," *Journal of Crime and Justice*, Vol. XV, No. 1, pp. 25–44.

Bureau of Justice Statistics. 1992a. *Drugs, Crime, and the Criminal Justice System: A National Report from the Bureau of Justice Statistics*, NCJ-133652, U.S. Government Printing Office, Washington, D.C.

Bureau of Justice Statistics. 1992b. *Federal Criminal Case Processing, 1982–91, with Preliminary Data for 1992*, United States Department of Justice, Washington, D.C.

Bureau of Justice Statistics. 1992c. *Felony Sentences in State Courts*, NCJ-151167, United States Department of Justice, Washington, D.C.

Bureau of Justice Statistics. 1993. *National Corrections Reporting Program, 1990*, Office of Justice Programs, U.S. Department of Justice, Washington, D.C.

Bureau of Justice Statistics. 1994. *Drugs and Crime Facts, 1993*, NCT-146246, United States Department of Justice, Washington, D.C.

Bureau of the Census. 1995. *Statistical Abstract of the United States: 1995* (115th edition), Washington, D.C.

Caulkins, Jonathan P. 1990. *The Distribution and Consumption of Illicit Drugs: Some Mathematical Models and Their Policy Implications*, Ph.D. Dissertation, Massachusetts Institute of Technology, May, Cambridge, Mass.

Caulkins, Jonathan P. 1994. *Developing Price Series for Cocaine*, MR-317-DPRC, RAND, Santa Monica, Calif.

Caulkins, Jonathan P. 1995. "Estimating Elasticities of Demand for Cocaine and Heroin with DUF Data," in submission.

Caulkins, Jonathan P., Gordon Crawford, and Peter Reuter. 1993. "Simulation of Adaptive Response: A Model of Drug Interdiction," *Mathematical Computer Modeling*, Vol. 17, No. 2, January, pp. 37–52.

Caulkins, Jonathan P., Patricia A. Ebener, and Daniel F. McCaffrey. 1995. "Describing DAWN's Dominion," *Contemporary Drug Problems*, Vol. 22, No. 3, pp. 547–567.

Caulkins, Jonathan P., and Rema Padman. 1993. "Quantity Discounts and Quality Premia for Illicit Drugs," *Journal of the American Statistical Association*, Vol. 88, No. 423, pp. 748–757.

Cave, Jonathan A. K., and Peter Reuter. 1988. *The Interdictor's Lot: A Dynamic Model of the Market for Drug Smuggling Services*, N-2632-USDP, February 1988, RAND, Santa Monica, Calif.

Childress, Michael. 1994a. *A System Description of the Heroin Trade*, MR-234-A/DPRC, RAND, Santa Monica, Calif.

Childress, Michael. 1994b. *A System Description of the Marijuana Trade*, MR-235-A/DPRC, RAND, Santa Monica, Calif.

Cohen, Jacqueline, Daniel Nogin, Garrick Wallstrom, and Larry Wasserman. Forthcoming. "Hierarchical Bayesian Analysis of Arrest Rates."

Cohen, Mark A. 1994. *The Monetary Value of Saving a High Risk Youth*, Report submitted to the Urban Institute, Vanderbilt University, Nashville, Tenn.

Cohen, Mark A., Ted R. Miller, and Shelli B. Rossman. 1994. "The Costs and Consequences of Violent Behavior in the United States," *Understanding and Preventing Violence: Volume 4—Consequences and Control*, Albert J. Reiss, and Jeffrey A. Roth, eds., National Academy Press, Washington, D.C., pp. 67–166.

Countywide Criminal Justice Coordination Committee. 1995. *Impact of the "Three Strikes Law" on the Criminal Justice System in Los Angeles County*, County of Los Angeles, Los Angeles, Calif.

Crawford, Gordon B., and Peter Reuter. 1988. *Simulation of Adaptive Response: A Model of Drug Interdiction*, N-2680-USDP, February 1988, RAND, Santa Monica, Calif.

Dembo, Richard, ed. 1994. "Drugs and Crime Revisited," *Journal of Drug Issues*, special issue, Vol. 24, No. 1 & 2.

DiNardo, John, and Thomas Lemieux. 1992. "Alcohol, Marijuana, and American Youth: The Unintended Consequences of Government Regulation," National Bureau of Economic Research, Working Paper No. 4212.

Dombey-Moore, Bonnie, and Susan Resetar. 1994. *A Systems Description of the Cocaine Trade*, MR-236-A/AF/DPRC, RAND, Santa Monica, Calif.

Everingham, Susan S., and C. Peter Rydell. 1994. *Modeling the Demand for Cocaine*, MR-332-ONDCP/A/DPRC, RAND, Santa Monica, Calif.

Federal Bureau of Investigation (FBI). 1992. *Uniform Crime Reports for the United States, 1991*, United States Department of Justice, U.S. Government Printing Office, Washington, D.C.

Fisher, Ann, Lauraine G. Chestnut, and Daniel M. Violette. 1989. "The Value of Reducing the Risks of Death: A Note on New Evidence," *Journal of Policy Analysis and Management*, Vol. 8, No. 1, pp. 88–100.

Flanagan, Timothy J., and Kathleen Maguire, eds. 1992. *Sourcebook of Criminal Justice Statistics: 1991*, U.S. Government Printing Office, Washington, D.C.

Forst, Brian. 1995. "Prosecution and Sentencing," *Crime*, James Q. Wilson and Joan Petersilia, eds., Institute for Contemporary Studies, San Francisco, Calif., pp. 363–386.

Frank, Richard S. 1987. "Drugs of Abuse: Data Collection Systems of DEA and Recent Trends," *Journal of Analytical Toxicology*, Vol. 11, Nov./Dec., pp. 237–241.

Gardiner, L. Keith, and Raymond C. Shreckengost. 1987. "A System Dynamics Model for Estimating Heroin Imports into the United States," *System Dynamics Review*, Vol. 3, No. 1, Winter, pp. 8–27.

Gawin, Frank H., and Everett H. Ellinwood. 1988. "Cocaine and Other Stimulants: Actions, Abuse, and Treatment," *New England Journal of Medicine*, Vol. 318, No. 18, May, pp. 1173–1182.

General Accounting Office. 1993. *Mandatory Minimum Sentences: Are They Being Imposed and Who Is Receiving Them?* GAO/GGD-94-13, November.

Gerstein, Dean R., and Henrick J. Harwood, eds. 1990. *Treating Drug Problems, Volume 1: A Study of the Evolution, Effectiveness, and Financing of Public and Private Drug Treatment Systems*, National Academy Press, Washington, D.C.

Goldstein, Paul J. 1985. "The Drugs/Violence Nexus: A Tripartite Conceptual Framework," *Journal of Drug Issues*, Fall.

Goldstein, Paul J., Henry H. Brownstein, and Patrick J. Ryan. 1992. "Drug-Related Homicide in New York: 1984 and 1988." *Crime and Delinquency*, Vol. 38, No. 4, pp. 459–476.

Goldstein, Paul J., Henry H. Brownstein, Patrick J. Ryan, and Patricia A. Bellucci. 1989. "Crack and Homicide in New York City, 1988: A Conceptually Based Event Analysis," *Contemporary Drug Problems*, Winter, pp. 651–687.

Goldstein, Paul J., Patricia A. Bellucci, Barry J. Spunt, and Thomas Miller. 1991. "Volume of Cocaine Use and Violence: A Comparison Between Men and Women," *Journal of Drug Issues*, Vol. 21, No. 2, pp. 345–367.

Greenwood, Peter W., C. Peter Rydell, Allan F. Abrahamse, Jonathan P. Caulkins, James Chiesa, Karyn E. Model, and Stephen P. Klein. 1994. *Three Strikes and You're Out: Estimated Benefits and Costs of California's New Mandatory Sentencing Law*, MR-509-RC, RAND, Santa Monica, Calif.

Grossman, Michael, Frank J. Chaloupka, and Charles C. Brown. 1996. *The Demand for Cocaine by Young Adults: A Rational Addiction Approach*, Working Paper No. 5713, August, National Bureau of Economic Research.

Harlow, C. W. 1992. *Drug Enforcement and Treatment in Prisons, 1990*. Bureau of Justice Statistics Special Report NCJ-134724, U.S. Government Printing Office, Washington, D.C.

Hatch, Orrin G. 1993. "The Role of Congress in Sentencing: The United States Sentencing Commission, Mandatory Minimum Sentences, and the Search for a Certain and Effective Sentencing System," *Wake Forest Law Review*, Vol. 28, pp. 185–198.

Homer, Jack B. 1990. *A System Dynamics Simulation Model of Cocaine Prevalence*, February, UCLA Drug Abuse Research Group, Los Angeles, Calif.

Homer, Jack B. 1993a. "A System Dynamics Model for Cocaine Prevalence Estimation and Trend Projection," *The Journal of Drug Issues*, Vol. 23, No. 2, Spring, pp. 251–279.

Homer, Jack B. 1993b. "Projecting the Impact of Law Enforcement on Cocaine Prevalence: A System Dynamics Approach," *The Journal of Drug Issues*, Vol. 23, No. 2, Spring, pp. 281–295.

Keeler, E. B., and S. Cretin. 1983. Discounting of Life-Saving and Other Nonmonetary Effects, *Management Science*, Vol. 29, pp. 300–306.

Kennedy, Michael, Peter Reuter, and Kevin Jack Riley. 1993. "A Simple Economic Model of Cocaine Production," *Mathematical and Computer Modelling*, Vol. 17, No. 2.

Kennedy, Michael, Peter Reuter, and Kevin Jack Riley. 1994. *A Simple Economic Model of Cocaine Production*, MR-201-USDP, RAND, Santa Monica, Calif.

Kleiman, Mark A. R. 1992. *Against Excess: Drug Policy for Results*, Basic Books, New York, N.Y.

Leiter, Richard A., ed. 1993. *National Survey of State Laws, First Edition*, Gale Research Inc., Detroit, Mich.

Levin, Gilbert, Edward B. Roberts, and Gary B. Hirsch. 1975. *The Persistent Poppy: A Computer-Aided Search for Heroin Policy*, Ballinger Publishing Company, Cambridge, Mass.

Maguire, Kathleen, and Ann L. Pastore, eds. 1994. *Sourcebook of Criminal Justice Statistics—1993*, U.S. Department of Justice, Bureau of Justice Statistics, U.S. Government Printing Office, Washington, D.C.

Maguire, Kathleen, and Ann L. Pastore, eds. 1995. *Sourcebook of Criminal Justice Statistics—1994*, U.S. Department of Justice, Bureau of Justice Statistics, U.S. Government Printing Office, Washington, D.C.

Manning, Willard G., Emmett B. Keeler, Joseph P. Newhouse, Elizabeth M. Sloss, and Jeffrey Wasserman. 1991. *The Costs of Poor Health Habits*, Harvard University Press, Cambridge, Mass.

McGlothlin, William, Kay Jamison, and Steven Rosenblatt. 1970. "Marijuana and the Use of Other Drugs," *Nature*, Vol. 228, pp. 1227–1229.

Model, Karyn E. 1992. *Economic Models of Drug and Alcohol Control Policy*, Ph.D. Dissertation, Harvard University, Cambridge, Mass.

Model, Karyn E. 1993. "The Effect of Marijuana Decriminalization on Hospital Emergency Room Drug Episodes: 1975–1978." *The Journal of the American Statistical Association*, Vol. 88, No. 423, pp. 737–747.

Musto, David F. 1973. *The American Disease*, Yale University Press, New Haven, Conn.

Musto, David F. 1989. "America's First Cocaine Epidemic," *The Wilson Quarterly*, Vol. 13, No. 3, Summer, pp. 59–64.

Musto, David F. 1991. "Opium, Cocaine, and Marijuana in American History," *Scientific American*, July, pp. 40–47.

National Drug Control Strategy. 1995. The White House, Washington, D.C.

National Drug Control Strategy Budget Summary. 1995. The White House, Washington, D.C.

National Institute of Justice. 1993. "Drug Use Forecasting: 1992 Annual Report," *Research in Brief,* NCJ-142973, May.

Office of National Drug Control Policy (ONDCP). 1992. *National Drug Control Strategy: Budget Summary,* The White House, Washington, D.C.

Office of National Drug Control Policy (ONDCP). 1993. *State and Local Spending on Drug Control Activities: Report from the National Survey of State and Local Governments,* The White House, Washington, D.C.

Office of National Drug Control Policy (ONDCP). 1995. *National Drug Control Strategy,* The White House, Washington, D.C.

Office of National Drug Control Policy (ONDCP). 1996. *National Drug Control Strategy,* The White House, Washington, D.C.

Perkins, Craig. 1993. *National Corrections Reporting Program–1990,* U.S. Department of Justice, Bureau of Justice Statistics, U.S. Government Printing Office, Washington, D.C.

Reuter, Peter. 1983. *Disorganized Crime,* MIT Press, Cambridge, Mass.

Reuter, Peter. 1992. "Hawks Ascendant: The Punitive Trend of American Drug Policy," *Daedalus,* Vol. 121, No. 3, Summer, pp. 15–52.

Reuter, Peter. 1994. "Setting Priorities: Budget and Program Choice for Drug Control," *Toward a Rational Drug Policy, the University of Chicago Legal Forum,* Vol. 1994, pp. 145–173.

Reuter, Peter, and Mark Kleiman. 1986. "Risks and Prices: An Economic Analysis of Drug Enforcement," *Crime and Justice: A Review of Research,* Norval Morris and Michael Tonry, eds., University of Chicago Press, Chicago, Ill., pp. 289–340.

Reuter, Peter, Robert MacCoun, and Patrick Murphy. 1990. *Money from Crime: A Study of the Economics of Drug Dealing in Washington, D.C.*, R-3894-RF, RAND, Santa Monica, Calif.

Rhodes, William, Paul Scheiman, Tanutda Pittayathikhun, Laura Collins, and Vered Tsarfaty. 1995. *What America's Users Spend on Illegal Drugs, 1988–1993*, Office of National Drug Control Policy, Washington, D.C.

Rice, Dorothy P., Sander Kelman, Leonard S. Miller, and Sarah Dunmeyer. 1990. *The Economic Costs of Alcohol and Drug Abuse and Mental Illness: 1985*, report submitted to the Office of Financing and Coverage Policy of the Alcohol, Drug Abuse, and Mental Health Administration, U.S. Department of Health and Human Services, Institute for Health and Aging, University of California, San Francisco, Calif.

Riley, Kevin Jack. 1993a. *Snow Job? The Efficacy of Source Country Cocaine Policies*, RGSD-102, RAND, Santa Monica, Calif.

Riley, Kevin Jack. 1993b. *Snow Job? The War Against International Cocaine Trafficking*, Transaction Publishers, Rutgers, N.J.

Rottenberg, Simon. 1968. "The Clandestine Distribution of Heroin, Its Discovery and Suppression," *Journal of Political Economy*, reprinted in *Microeconomics: Selected Readings*, 3rd Ed., Edwin Mansfield, ed., W. W. Norton & Co., New York, N.Y.

Ryan, Patrick J., Paul J. Goldstein, Henry H. Brownstein, and Patricia A. Bellucci. 1990. "Who's Right: Different Outcomes When Police and Scientists View the Same Set of Homicide Events, New York City, 1988." *Drugs and Violence: Causes, Correlates, and Consequences*, Mario De La Rosa, Elizabeth Y. Lambert, and Bernard Gropper, eds., NIDA Research Monograph 103, U.S. Department of Health and Human Services, Rockville, Md.

Rydell, C. Peter, and Susan S. Everingham. 1994. *Controlling Cocaine: Supply Versus Demand Programs*, MR-331-ONDCP/A/DPRC, RAND, Santa Monica, Calif.

Saffer, Henry, and Frank Chaloupka. 1995. *The Demand for Illicit Drugs*, Working Paper No. 5238, National Bureau of Economic Research, Cambridge, Mass.

Schlenger, William E. 1973. "A Systems Approach to Drug User Services," *Behavioral Science*, Vol. 18, No. 2, pp. 137–147.

Schulhofer, Stephen J. 1993. "Rethinking Mandatory Minimums," *Wake Forest Law Review*, Vol. 28, pp. 199–222.

Scotkin, Ronnie M. 1989. "The Development of the Federal Sentencing Guideline for Drug Trafficking Offenses," *Criminal Law Bulletin*, pp. 50–59.

Spunt, Barry J., Paul J. Goldstein, Patricia A. Bellucci, and Thomas Miller. 1990. "Race/Ethnicity and Gender Differences in the Drugs-Violence Relationship," *Journal of Psychoactive Drugs*, Vol. 22, No. 3, pp. 293–303.

Spunt, Barry, Henry Brownstein, Paul Goldstein, Michael Fendrich, and Hilary James Liberty. 1995. "Drug Use by Homicide Offenders," *Journal of Psychoactive Drugs*, Vol. 27, No. 2, pp. 125–134.

United States Sentencing Commission. 1991. *Mandatory Minimum Penalties in the Federal Criminal Justice System*, special report to the Congress, August.

Van Ours, Jan C. 1995. "The Price Elasticity of Hard Drugs: The Case of Opium in the Dutch East Indies, 1923–1938," *Journal of Political Economy*, Vol. 103, No. 2, pp. 261–279.

Zimring, Franklin E., and Gordon Hawkins. 1995. *Incapacitation: Penal Confinement and the Restraint of Crime*, Oxford University Press, New York, N.Y.